The One True God –
His Characteristics and Names

*A Daily Devotional on getting to know and love
the One True God -
by studying His Characteristics and Names*

by Gini Crawford (MSW)

For a child will be born to us, a son will be given to us; and the government will rest on His shoulders; and His name will be called Wonderful Counselor, Mighty God, Eternal Father, Prince of Peace.
Isaiah 9:6

The One True God - His Characteristics and Names

The One True God – His Characteristics and Names

Thus says the LORD,

"Let not a wise man boast of his wisdom,
and let not the mighty man boast of his might,
let not a rich man boast of his riches;
but let him who boasts boast of this,
that he understands and knows Me..."
Jeremiah 9:23-24a

"What commandment is the foremost of all?"
Jesus answered, "The foremost is,

'HEAR, O ISRAEL! THE LORD OUR
GOD IS ONE LORD;
AND YOU SHALL LOVE THE LORD
YOUR GOD WITH ALL YOUR HEART,
AND WITH ALL YOUR SOUL,
AND WITH ALL YOUR MIND,
AND WITH ALL YOUR STRENGTH.'"
Mark 12:28b-30

To my husband, Tom Crawford,
who is always there for me.
He edits my writings
and keeps the Because of God Ministries website
(BecauseofGod.com) up and running.
He sacrificially does this as he
runs a physics consulting business.

To my daughter, Ruth McClung,
who always tells me, "Mom, you can do that."
when I am doubting myself.

Table of Contents

Introduction

I have had a number of people ask me if I was going to write a study on God's characteristics for my website. To be honest, I thought I didn't have the time, so I would say no. But God always seems to change my plans so His plans get done. A friend of mine said, "I would have become a Christian many years ago, if I had known God was real and so loving. Sorry I wasted so many years on thinking He wasn't real. How foolish was that?" I believe we can all feel like we could have been learning more about God, sooner and in more ways. Well, now you have another chance. God literally cleared my schedule to write this.

As you can see from the teachings on BecauseOfGod.com, I describe God every chance I get. Why do I do this? When you get to know some people, you wish you had not. Sadly, I bet you can relate. But God is the opposite - the more we know God, the more we want to know Him, love Him, and trust Him. So frankly, I loved writing this Daily Devotional on God's characteristics and names. It has allowed me to get to know my loving and amazing God even better.

The One True God – His Characteristics and Names is a 33 day devotional. Each day teaches about one or two characteristics and/or a name of God. The devotional covers 24 characteristics and 12 names of God, and touches on others with less detail. It uses many Bible passages to substantiate the commentary, and it uses a number of meaningful and amusing illustrations. It teaches what each name or characteristic means, where it is found in the Bible, and how to personally and practically apply it.

How to use this book

Daily or weekly: This daily devotional is setup in an eight week format so you can either do it daily or weekly.

Nine week group study format: I have been asked to modify this 33 day devotional for use in Group Bible Studies. For this, I have broken the devotional down into a nine week format with extra questions and insights to help facilitate a good group discussion. *See pages 198-220, if you are doing this as a group study.*

One day a week: A friend told me she did this devotional at the pace of one day each week. This gave her time to mediate on each characteristic or name of God and the related Bible passages. Each day can also be used as a separate devotion for an event. A weekly prayer group used this devotional over 33 weeks for their group devotional time.

In this daily devotional, *The One True God – His Characteristics and Names*, I have used numerous Bible passages, so you can understand the One True God from His book, the Jewish (Old Testament) and Christian (New Testament) Scriptures, called the Bible. Because of the amount of quoted Bible passages, for room sake, I had to cut some words or verses out; so if you have time please re-read the whole passage in your Bible. (Others who have done this devotional tell me it flows easier if you stay with the Bible translation I am using - the New American Standard Bible 1995).

This book is written so you can apply the information as you read. The Life Application section at the end of each day gives you extra information. I have left plenty of room throughout the book to write down your insights on each day. Each day will take around 20 minutes or more - depending on how many Bible passages you look up, the length of the Bible readings, and how much you study. Please start each devotional asking God to teach you about Himself.

Look at the birds of the air, that they do not sow, nor reap nor gather into barns, and yet your heavenly Father feeds them. Are you not worth much more than they? Matthew 6:26

The One True God - His Characteristics and Names

Week One

Days One through Four

~Notes~

You Must Know the One True God
~Day One~

I would imagine many of you are interested in this daily devotional on God's characteristics and names because you already know the One True God but want a better understanding of Him. Maybe some of you are just fascinated with what someone would teach about the One True God. But whatever your reason, I am glad you are taking the time to do it. You will not regret it.

I believe you are not doing this devotional by accident. God led you to this book, to yes, get to know Him, but maybe for another reason that only He knows.

In this devotional you will learn such things as:
- Who the One True God is through His characteristics and names.
- Who Jesus Christ really is.
- Why our world is full of suffering, even though God the Creator made everything good.
- God is the source of all life, but He took on death so you could have life again.
- What is the Trinity?
- The real meaning of heaven.
- God is the Self-Existent One who needs no one, but still wants to communicate with you and to love you.
- How personal and loving the One True God is.

Knowing the right God

Many people throughout the world believe in a god or in multiple gods, but they don't believe in the One True God as He revealed Himself in the Jewish and Christian Scriptures, called the Bible. And how can you believe in the right God if you don't know Him?

Some of you might be thinking now, "What does she mean by the 'One True God'? Aren't all gods the same? Is there really a One True God?" We can all struggle with who the One True God is. I have. In effect, all other gods are the same because they are conceived by humans; but the One True God is different. He is the One Who brought forth our existence and everything else in existence, and sustains that existence. God is the Self-Existent One, Who astonishingly created us to love us and have a relationship with us. I have been a Christian for decades, and I am still amazed daily on how exalted but personal our God is.

> *...So that you may know and believe Me. And understand that I am He. Before Me there was no God formed, and there will be none after Me. "I, even I, am the LORD, and there is no savior besides Me." Isaiah 43:10-11 (NASB)*

<u>Why is it so important to know the One True God?</u> The One True God is the only god that gives the certainty of eternal life. Therefore, knowing and consequently believing in the One True God determines where you go after death. I believe we all want that assurance.

This is eternal life, that they may know You, the only true God, and Jesus Christ whom You have sent. / For God so loved the world, that He gave His only begotten Son (Jesus Christ), that whoever believes in Him shall not perish, but have eternal life. John 17:3, 3:16 (NASB)

There are books and shows out there that fictionally portray the One True God. Since some of these are popular, it demonstrates people are interested in God. This is a good thing. However, it is very counterproductive to your Christian faith as well as your eternity if your information about God is incorrect. Knowing God, like Daniel in the Old Testament did, is so important.[1] That's why in this daily devotional, I describe God from many Bible passages, so that you can read and study for yourself Who God really is.

Daniel said, "Let the name of God be blessed forever and ever, for wisdom and power belong to Him. It is He who changes the times and the epochs; He removes kings and establishes kings; He gives wisdom to wise men and knowledge to men of understanding. It is He who reveals the profound and hidden things; He knows what is in the darkness, and the light dwells with Him." Daniel 2:20-22 (NASB)

Is knowing and understanding the One True God important to you? I would imagine it is, because you are taking the time to do this devotional.

~Life Application~

God's true happily ever after story

Many of our favorite movies and books have happily ever after endings. These endings come about because good conquers evil, and true love wins the day. A happily ever after story that was in theatres when I began to write this was the new Disney movie, *Beauty and the Beast*. (Honestly, I have ended up watching this movie three times.) These happily ever after stories are thought of as enchanted make believe tales.

What many people don't realize, or maybe just do not understand, is that the One True God did create us all to live happily ever after. God's true story goes like this: Millenniums ago in the beginning of time, the One True God personally created the very good world for humankind to live forever in. However, evil temporarily triumphed since Adam and Eve chose the evil villain, Satan, over the loving Creator. But not all was lost. The One True God had an eternal plan to conquer evil, so His true love for us can reign without end; and of course, we will live happily ever after with Him. If you are wondering where I found this beautiful tale as old as time, well it is found in God's Book, the Bible, which is as true as time itself.

This true happily ever after story about the One True God is just the beginning. There is so much more to learn about God. Each day in this devotional, you will cover a topic or two about God; so that by the end of the 33 days, you will have an all-encompassing picture in your mind of Who the One True God really is. If you are diligent to read and look up all the Bible verses in this devotional, your view of God will be heading in the right direction.

Write out a sentence committing to prayerfully complete this daily devotional on Who the One True God is.

Exhortation: The One True God is asking you to learn of Him, so you will have life eternal with Him.

Thinking of God Rightly
~Day Two~

Don't worship a false image

In a popular novel, God is made out to be a very friendly woman. I think many of you realize that to describe God this way is completely unbiblical. I have also heard people say, "This story makes me crave God's presence." There is a problem with this, because they are yearning over a man-made image of God, instead of yearning after God Himself. To make God out to be someone He is not, is what the Ten Commandments tell us not to do.

> *You shall have no other gods before Me. You shall not make for yourself an idol, or any likeness of what is in heaven above or on the earth beneath or in the water under the earth. You shall not worship them or serve them; for I, the LORD your God, am a jealous God... Deuteronomy 5:7-9 (NASB)*

The One True God is zealous that devotion be given exclusively to Him, and not to a false image of Him. Wouldn't it be disheartening to have people not to like or love you for who you are, so they make up a fictitious you? My family wanted me to be different than I was, but at least they didn't make up a pretend child. Don't create God by your or someone else's preconceived ideas. Believe me, after years of knowing and studying God from His Word, I guarantee He is so much more wonderful than what anyone could make up.

To know God's Word is to think rightly of God

We can all have ideas of Who God is that are contrary to His Word. Before I started reading and studying the Bible, I used to think of God as a nice man, in a white flowing robe, who always had to sit down because he was so old. Believe me, that view of God didn't help me. God wants us to know the real Him, not a man-made idea of Him. The only place that you can find the real God is through His Word, the Bible. Other books can surely explain the One True God rightly, if their understanding of God comes from His Word.

Where do you go to get to know the One True God? Do you go to God's own words, the Bible, or to some person's writing?

Understanding God brings strength

The closer our understanding of God is to the truth, the stronger Christians we will be (Ephesians 3:17-19, 4:13-16; 2 Timothy 3:16-17). Let me explain this through a few examples. If you don't think of God as holy, then you will likely think you can sin (or disobey God) and He won't care. This is not true, because God is holy, just, and righteous so He hates sin, and will not tolerate sin. If you think of God as a friendly human, then you will treat Him like a person. Yes, God does want to be our best friend, but He is so much more than that. This type of god can't save you, or empower you because he is on your level. Do you really want to serve and worship a god like you?

Do you know if your view of God is right?

Thinking of God rightly will give you the desire to believe in Him, and as a result you will have eternal life. It will make you want to know His every single word to you, like a love letter. It will give you the longing to love, and serve Him. It will literally make you want to fall down on your knees and worship Him, as well as dream of the day you will be able to talk to Him face to face.

~Life Application~

Dangers of worshipping a false image

The book of Exodus in the Old Testament, is a very good example of how important it is to God to think of Him rightly. In Exodus, the One True God revealed Himself to the nation of Israel through signs and wonders, His presence leading them day and night, and a number of them seeing Him (Jesus Christ) in His glory. (Exodus 13:20-22, 14:21-31, 24:9-11 also John 1:18).

Even though Israel experienced God's miracles and presence, they still disobeyed God, and made a golden image of Him in the form of a calf to worship. God's anger burned against them because He had clearly revealed Himself to them, and had just told them not to make a false image of Him; which they heartily agreed to. *Read Exodus 19:2-8, 20:18-23, 24:9-18, 32:1-14, 19-24, 31-35.* Here are some other passages on creating a false image of God and worshipping it. *Read Isaiah 44:14-17; Romans 1:18-25.*

How do you think of God? Be honest.

What have you learned about the dangers or futility of creating a false god and giving that god your devotion?

Who should you give your devotion too? *Read Romans 5:8-10; 1 John 5:20.*

God's Characteristics Introduced
~Day Three~

Defining God's characteristics

I learned in graduate school to define important words, so let's define the meaning of God's characteristics. The One True God's characteristics are whatever He has in any way revealed as being true about Himself through His Word. His characteristics as well as His names describe Who He is. It is vital we know that all God's characteristics and names fill His whole being and act together. God isn't somewhat powerful, He is all-powerful. He isn't kind of knowledgeable, He is all-knowing, and so on.

Scholars differ on the number of God's characteristics. The characteristics I will cover, are the ones many religious leaders understand and teach on. These characteristics of God are: self-existence, all-powerful, eternal, the source of life, sovereign, holy, righteous, just, merciful, good, patient, full of grace, unchanging, faithful, truthful/true, all-knowing, all-wise, always with you, all-seeing, all-hearing, incomprehensible, kind, forgiving, and all-loving. I will cover in depth some of God's most notable names: Jesus Christ, God the Father, God the Son, God the Holy Spirit, Creator, LORD, I AM, Father, Husband, Savior, Servant, Lamb, and Shepherd, as well as a few other lesser known names.

God has two types of attributes or characteristics. They are called incommunicable and communicable attributes.[1] The communicable attributes of God are the ones that we have because we are created in God's image. They are such things as a personality marked with emotions, moral character, the desire for relationship, the desire to be loved and to love, the capacity to have patience, wisdom, mercy, justice, goodness and faithfulness, and so on. We also have an eternal existence that began when God created us. The incommunicable attributes of God are the ones only God can have. These include such things as being self-existent, the source of all life, always seeing, always present, and so on. As I teach God's characteristics, both types will be used to enlighten and inspire.

It's good to understand we have the communicable attributes that God has given us, but they are never to the degree that God has them. We are loving and have wisdom and knowledge, but of course, we will never always be as loving or have all wisdom or knowledge like God does.

Knowing God

God knows you, and wants you to know Him (Psalm 139:1-4). This is an amazing reality, isn't it? So you need to not just know of God, but to really know Him. I know of the President of the United States; but I really know my husband, Tom, who I have been married to for over 40 years. God wants to be known as I know my husband.

Thus says the LORD, *"Let not a wise man boast of his wisdom, and let not the mighty man boast of his might, let not a rich man boast of his riches; but let him who boasts boast of this, that he understands and knows Me, that I am the* LORD *who exercises lovingkindness, justice and righteousness on earth; for I delight in these things,"* declares the LORD. *Jeremiah 9:23-24 (NASB)*

Do you just know of God, or do you really know Him? I guarantee you - the more you get to know God, the more you will want to know Him, as well as to love and serve Him.

~*Life Application*~

Knowing God, like Daniel in the Old Testament

Daniel will be used throughout this devotional, to give an example of a person who truly knew and loved the One True God. So let's start getting familiar with Daniel.

The second chapter of the book of Daniel (written by Daniel) is a dream from God that summarizes the world's future empires. This chapter also explains how the One True God saved all the wise men in Babylon from King Nebuchadnezzar, who was going to execute them because they couldn't interpret his dream. Daniel prayed to God, Who revealed to Daniel what no human could know, the king's dream. *Read Daniel 2:17-49.*

Describe God from this passage.

What did you learn about Daniel that you want to exemplify
in your life?

How did Daniel chapter two personally speak to you?

Daniel chapter four is again about a dream from God, but this time it was to warn a proud king. King Nebuchadnezzar is the evil tyrant in Daniel chapter two, but as you will see in chapter four, God can change the most evil person for the good. This chapter tells a true story of how the most powerful man in the world at the time (King Nebuchadnezzar of Babylon), learned Who the One True God really is and to be humble before Him. *Read Daniel 4: 1-9, 19-37.*

Describe God from this passage.

How did Daniel chapter four personally speak to you?

This story always reminds me, I need to be humble (the opposite of pride, dependence on God not self) before God, and if I am not, who knows what drastic happenings will come my way. Honestly, if you want to be right with God, being humble is a must (1 Peter 5:5-6).

Exhortation: Knowing Who God really is
will change your life in
real and wonderful ways.

The One True God and the Trinity
~Day Four~

The Trinity introduced

The doctrine or principle of the Trinity is - God is One God, but He exists eternally in three persons; each person is fully God. God's Word teaches us the One True God is: God the Father, God the Son and God the Holy Spirit. The word trinity is never used in the Bible. It is a man-made technical term used to define the foundational truth of Who God is.[1]

Have you ever heard of the Trinity? When I first became a Christian, I was taught about the Trinity, and just kind of took it on faith. However as I became more familiar with the Bible, I began to see God being One but in three persons all throughout it.

I think the idea of the Trinity is difficult for us to comprehend *fully* because our reasoning is from an earthly perspective. But we need to remember, God is God! He is incomprehensible. His ways, His thoughts, His reasoning, His power, His love, and so on, are so far above ours. Why wouldn't He be three persons, since He is so much greater in all ways than we are? In Isaiah 55:8-9 God states,

> *"For My thoughts are not your thoughts, nor are your ways My ways," declares the LORD. "For as the heavens are higher than the earth, so are My ways higher than your ways, and My thoughts than your thoughts."*
> *Isaiah 55:8-9 (NASB)*

God the Son

God the Son, who is Jesus Christ, explains the One True God to us. In God the Son - the word son or *huios* in the Greek language means relationship of Son to Father, or likeness of character, but never birth.[2] God the Father is Spirit, so no man has seen Him at anytime (John 4:24). The New Testament, very plainly teaches that Jesus has revealed God to us - He is God in flesh. Jesus said in John 14:9, *"he who has seen Me has seen the Father."* Many places in the Bible it is hard to tell whether the passage is talking about God the Father or God the Son. This is because of the doctrine of the Trinity.

> *No one has seen God at any time; the only begotten God who is in the bosom of the Father, He has explained Him. John 1:18 (NASB)*

Jesus Christ physically shows God to us (John 14:7-11; Colossians 2:9). Jesus was in the Garden of Eden talking to Adam and Eve. He appeared to Hagar in Genesis chapter sixteen as the angel of the LORD; He appeared a number of other times to other people. Temporary appearances by God the Son to humans are called theophanies, which occurred before His incarnation.[3]

The incarnation of Jesus Christ took place about 2,000 years ago, when God the Son willingly let go of His glory and rights as the One True God, to take on flesh and blood. Jesus became a human just like you and me, but He was very different too. This was because He was conceived by the Holy Spirit, which meant He was still fully God and had no sin nature. As He lived on this earth, He had the same hardships and joys poor people back then had. He also had the weaknesses, needs, temptations, and ills we all do. He also chose to suffer in ways no one else ever did for our sakes. Yet through it all He never sinned. Since He is God, He had to temporarily surrender His eternal nature to die on a cross for our sins. (Matthew 1:18-25; Philippians 2:6-8; Hebrews 4:14-16). The Son of God did all of this so we could live happily ever after with Him. Incredible God, isn't He?

> For a child will be born to us, a son will be given to us... And His name will be called Wonderful Counselor, Mighty God, Eternal Father, Prince of Peace. Isaiah 9:6 (NASB)

What does it mean to you that Jesus Christ is the One True God?

God the Holy Spirit

God the Holy Spirit is also called the Spirit of truth. He is our Helper (Counselor). He represents Jesus to us. This is because He is Jesus Christ's proxy in the world while Jesus isn't here in bodily form. Jesus' disciples were worried about Him leaving them, so Jesus tells them about His Helper, the Holy Spirit. He assures them that His Helper will be sent to them and will live within them - to guide, comfort, empower, and teach them (and us too).[4]
(John 14:16-17, 26, 16:13-15; Acts 1:8).

As a Christian, did you know you have a hotline to God because His Spirit lives within you? What does it mean to you that the Holy Spirit is your Helper?

~Life Application~

The Triune God

Today we learned about a fundamental doctrine - God is One but eternally exists in three persons. Look up and read each of these passages from God's Word which describe the fact of the Trinity. Write down one insight for each section.

- God is One God: *Read Isaiah 45:5-6, 21-22; Deuteronomy 6:4-5 also Mark 12:29-30; Matthew 28:19.*

- Jesus is God in the Old Testament: *Read Isaiah 9:6; Isaiah 7:14 also Matthew 1:23 (Immanuel* means God with us).

- Jesus is God in the New Testament: *Read John 1:18; John 14:7-11; 2 Corinthians 4:4; Philippians 2:6; Colossians 1:15,19-20, 2:9; Hebrews 1:3; 1 John 5:20.*

- The Holy Spirit is God: *Read Exodus 31:3; Isaiah 11:2; John 16:13-15; Acts 5:3-4; Romans 8:9-11.* 7-11

The sinful nature is always hostile to God. It never did obey God's laws, and it never will. That's why those who are still under the control of their sinful nature can never (please God.

But you are not controlled by your sinful nature. You are controlled by the Spirit if you have the Spirit of Christ living in you. And remember that those who do not have the

(And remember that those who do not have the Spirit of Christ living in them do not belong to Him at all.)

Exhortation: Let the Triune God's presence love you and guide you.

The One True God - His Characteristics and Names

20

Week Two

Days Five through Eight

Day 5. God the Creator
Day 6. God is the LORD, I AM, the Self-Existent One
Day 7. The One True God is All-Powerful
Day 8. God is Eternal, the Source of Life

~Notes~

Songs of Praise for Salvation

1) Song of Deliverance
(Exodus from Egypt)

(Moses & the people of Israel)

Exodus 15:2 -
"The Lord is my strength and my song; He has given me Victory. This is my God and I will praise Him.

3)
(Millennium)
vs. 12:6
Let all the people of Jerusalem shout His praise with joy! For great is the Holy One of Israel who lives among you.

Isaiah 12:2 - "God has come to save me. I will trust in Him and not be afraid. The LORD GOD is my strength and my song; He has given me Victory.

2) Psalm 118:13-15 My enemies did their best to kill me, but the LORD rescued me. The LORD is my strength and my song; He has given me Victory. Songs of joy and victory are sung in the camp of the godly. The strong right arm of the LORD has done glorious things!

Jesus' sacrifice for our sins! Rescued us from sin & death.

VS 22 - The Stone that the builders rejected has now become the Cornerstone.
VS 26 - Bless the one who comes in the name of the Lord.

God the Creator
~Day Five~

The One True God is the Creator

In the first book of the Bible, Genesis, in the first chapter, we are told God is the Creator.

> *In the beginning God created the heavens and the earth.*
> *Genesis 1:1 (NASB)*

In the first chapter of Romans in the New Testament, we are told we can see God's characteristics throughout His creation. Nowadays, many people worship nature. Yet in reality if you love nature, you are loving God's handiwork, His creation, whether you think so or not. One of my favorite things to do is to enjoy God as I walk in the wonder of His creation. How about you?

> *For since the creation of the world His invisible attributes,*
> *His eternal power and divine nature, have been clearly*
> *seen, being understood through what has been made...*
> *Romans 1:20a (NASB)*

As you travel the road of life, if you are willing to look, you will see God: When I watch my grandchildren, I play with God's amazing handiwork. The Japanese puffer fish surprisingly draws complicated designs in the sand with its fins, giving us a glimpse into God's intricate universe. When you look up into the sky at night, you see God's infinite power, knowledge and wisdom in each star. The sunrise shows God's goodness and faithfulness. People feel God's unconditional love and kindness in their children and pets.

Creation described

In Genesis chapter one, God spoke and our world was formed - light overcame the darkness; dry land and seas appeared; vegetation and trees flourished; birds, bugs, and animals small and large inhabited the earth, and so on (Hebrews 11:3). We also learn humans were created in God's image, creation was created very good, and God made us rulers over His creation (Psalm 8:3-8). Genesis chapter one is summarized below:

> *In the beginning God created the heavens and the earth...and the Spirit of God was moving over the surface of the waters. Then God said, "Let there be light"; and there was light. God saw that the light was good; and God separated the light from the darkness. God called the light day, and the darkness He called night... one day.*
>
> *Then God said, "Let there be an expanse in the midst of the waters, and let it separate the waters from the waters."... and it was so...God called the expanse heaven...a second day.*
>
> *Then God said, "Let the waters below the heavens be gathered into one place, and let the dry land appear"; and it was so. God called the dry land earth, and the gathering of the waters He called seas; and God saw that it was good. Then God said, "Let the earth sprout vegetation, plants yielding seed, and fruit trees on the earth bearing fruit after their kind with seed in them"; and it was so...and God saw that it was good...a third day.*

Then God said, "Let there be lights in the expanse of the heavens to separate the day from the night, and let them be for signs and for seasons and for days and years..." and it was so...God made the two great lights, the greater light to govern the day, and the lesser light to govern the night; He made the stars also. God placed them in the expanse of the heavens to give light on the earth, and to govern the day and the night, and to separate the light from the darkness; and God saw that it was good...a fourth day.

Then God said, "Let the waters teem with swarms of living creatures, and let birds fly above the earth in the open expanse of the heavens." God created the great sea monsters and every living creature that moves, with which the waters swarmed after their kind, and every winged bird after its kind; and God saw that it was good...a fifth day.

Then God said, "Let the earth bring forth living creatures after their kind: cattle and creeping things and beasts of the earth after their kind"; and it was so...and God saw that it was good.

Then God said, "Let Us make man in Our image, according to Our likeness; and let them rule over the fish of the sea and over the birds of the sky and over the cattle and over all the earth, and over every creeping thing that creeps on the earth." God created man in His own image, in the image of God He created him; male and female He created them. God blessed them; and God said to them, "Be fruitful and multiply..." God saw all that He had made, and behold, it was very good...the sixth day. (NASB)

The Creator

God has power and wisdom that are far beyond our human understanding (Jeremiah 10:12). As you saw in Genesis chapter one, God spoke and what He wanted to create literally appeared. Yet, God the Creator is so personal, He created you and me to personally love and care for. (Psalm 139:1-16; Jeremiah 31:3). Pretty amazing reality, isn't it?

The more I understand how vast and infinite the One True God is, the more I am surprised over His great desire to be so intimate with me. He knows and loves me so deeply that even when I get in a panic over something as minor as a bad hair day, He knows about it and cares. (Matthew 10:29-31; Luke 12:6-7; 1 John 3:1a). Why would anyone not want to get to know this God?

~Life Application~

The beginning of our world

In Genesis chapter one, God created everything that humans would need to live happily forever. He created all things thinking of what we needed and even wanted. Did you notice how God describes creation as *good*, then after people are created it is *very good*?

How does knowing God is your Creator influence your life?

<u>Genesis chapter two</u> explains in detail day six of creation, and gives the first command that had a consequence. *Read Genesis 2:1-10, 15-25.*

Write any insights you have from Genesis chapter two.

What was God's only command (Genesis 2:16-17) to Adam and Eve that they had to obey, or there would be an awful consequence? What was the consequence if not obeyed?

<u>Genesis chapter three</u> describes how sin came into the world. *Read Genesis 3:1-15.*

In Genesis 3:1, the serpent is the devil, also called Satan (2 Corinthians 11:3; Revelation 12:9).

In Genesis 3:8-9, the LORD God was walking in the garden looking for Adam and Eve to talk with them. These verses give us a beautiful glimpse into the intimacy God wants to have with us.

In Genesis 3:1-13 the sin of Adam and Eve is described. Even after they had sinned Jesus Christ was still in the garden with them, but things were changing. God created them (and all of us) to possess only life, good, pleasure, abundance, peace and harmony; but their sin brought death, evil, insecurity, pain, scarcity, toil, conflict and alienation into the world as well. Jesus' patience and mercy lovingly encouraged them to acknowledge their sin, but instead they were blaming each other, even Him, for their sin.

In Genesis 3:14-15, Jesus cursed the serpent and then gives the first hope of salvation, by describing a spiritual battle that He would triumph over to save His people (Colossians 1:13-20).

Why do you think Adam and Eve decided to disobey God?

How did Jesus Christ care for Adam and Eve after they had sinned against Him?

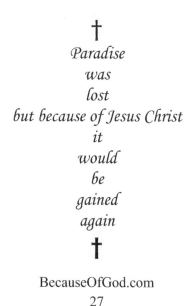

†

Paradise
was
lost
but because of Jesus Christ
it
would
be
gained
again

†

For since the creation of the world His invisible attributes, His eternal power and divine nature, have been clearly seen, being understood through what has been made, so that they are without excuse. Romans 1:20

The One True God - His Characteristics and Names

God is LORD, I AM, the Self-Existent One
~Day Six~

Explaining the LORD, I AM

Do bushes really talk? Remember the Bible story of Moses and the burning bush? In Exodus chapter three, the One True God remarkably talks through a burning bush, and tells Moses His formal name - I AM WHO I AM, or it could be translated, I am He Who exists. I AM is closely related to God's personal name Yahweh (Hebrew language). In English Bibles the word LORD (in all capitals) is Yahweh, and is used over 6,000 times in the Old Testament.[1]

LORD and I AM both emphasize God's self-existence. They also stress His power, timelessness and presence.[1]

> *"...So that you may know and believe Me, and understand that I am He. Before Me there was no God formed, and there will be none after Me. I, even I, am the LORD, and there is no savior besides Me ... And I am God. Even from eternity I am He, and there is none who can deliver out of My hand; I act and who can reverse it?" Isaiah 43:10-13 (NASB)*

It makes sense that the One True God is self-existent, doesn't it? Being self-existent means existence derived from itself, having no other source. God doesn't need any element of creation for His existence (Acts 17:24-28). God wasn't created but He is the Creator. Before the earth was formed or even before the beginning of time, the LORD existed (Psalm 90:2). God is the Self-Existent One.[2]

The LORD, I AM cares

The LORD, I AM, the Self-Existent One, created all life and needs no one – yet He incredibly wanted to talk to and share His divine name with the man, Moses, in Exodus chapter three. While talking, the LORD explained to Moses Who He is - that He is the God Who sees, hears, knows and will be with him. Together they would deliver His suffering people, and bring them to a prosperous land. Exodus 3:1-15 is summarized below.

> *Now Moses... led the flock to... the mountain of God. The angel of the LORD (Jesus Christ) appeared to him in a blazing fire from the midst of a bush... When the LORD saw that he turned aside to look, God called to him from the midst of the bush... Then He said, "Do not come near here ...for the place on which you are standing is holy ground..." Then Moses hid his face, for he was afraid to look at God. The LORD said, "I have surely seen the affliction of My people who are in Egypt, and have given heed to their cry because of their taskmasters, for I am aware of their sufferings. So I have come down to deliver them from the power of the Egyptians, and to bring them up from that land to a good and spacious land... Therefore, come now, and I will send you to Pharaoh, so that you may bring My people, the sons of Israel, out of Egypt." But Moses said to God, "Who am I... that I should bring the sons of Israel out of Egypt?" And He said, "Certainly I will be with you..." "Now they may say to me, 'What is His name?' What shall I say to them?" God said to Moses, "I AM WHO I AM"; and He said, "Thus you shall say to the sons of Israel, 'I AM has sent me to you.'" God, furthermore, said to Moses, "Thus you shall say to the sons of Israel, 'The LORD, the God of your fathers, the God of Abraham, the God of Isaac, and the God of Jacob, has sent me to you.' This is My name forever..." Exodus 3:1-15 (NASB)*

Jesus is the LORD, I AM

Jesus Christ is the LORD, I AM, Who needs no one, yet He died so you could be with Him. This is a life-changing truth for me. Is it for you? The Gospel of John in the New Testament, teaches us the wonderful truth of Jesus being our LORD, I AM (John 1:1-4, 14, 18, 8:23-24, 58, 14:6-9).

Jesus wants to talk to us, have a relationship with us and provide for us, as He did with Moses and the Israelites. Moses told God, "I can't deliver the people." God told him, "Yes you can because I AM is with you." When you see nothing but doubt, darkness or fear, and wonder if God is even there or near, remember Jesus is the great I AM - His presence and power are there with you.

As I was in the process of editing today's devotional, I went to our Post Office. A bewildered woman was standing there reading something, and looked up and said to me, "Can you explain what the LORD, I AM means?" This took me back because who asks a stranger that question? Then I realized the LORD had set this divine appointment up, and I answered, "Oh yes! It's what I have been writing about." What a remarkable meeting arranged by our great I AM. Jesus was there.

What are your thoughts on Jesus Christ being your LORD, I AM?

~Life Application~

The Self-Existent One and us

Read Exodus 3:1-15 again from your Bible if you have time. This passage explains God's formal name, but it also gives us a stunning view of Who God is.

Describe God from Exodus 3:1-15.

Did you notice in Exodus 3:1-15, how the LORD, I AM was determined to deliver His people from their suffering? What does this truth mean to you personally?

How did the LORD, I AM, the Self-Existent One, care for His people in Exodus chapter three?

How does He care for you?

An acquaintance told me a disheartening story about not being wanted. She told me, "I went to a small group at my church, and was told, 'We don't have room for you, so don't come back.'" I believe we all need to be wanted, so when we aren't, it hurts, doesn't it? God the Creator and Self-Existent One, chose to create us and love us, because He wanted us. You can't get more wanted by someone than that, can you? God being self-existent means He doesn't need anyone or anything to exist and to be complete. Yet, He wants me. Oh yes, I am very treasured and wanted by my God, and you are too.

Exhortation: Instead of being depressed or disheartened by your situation, ask the LORD, I AM, to give you His power and joy. He is with you.

The One True God is All-Powerful
~Day Seven~

God is omnipotent

Omnipotent means God is all-powerful (Jeremiah 16:21). God spoke and the power of the universe went forth - the heavens and earth were created, the sun and moon appeared, the mountains and oceans were formed, the birds, fish and animals took shape, we were created, and so on. When I think God spoke the universe and our world into being without lifting a finger, I am dumbfounded with such power. How about you?

> *...For wisdom and power belong to Him. / ...Saying, 'My purpose will be established, and I will accomplish all My good pleasure...' Daniel 2:20b; Isaiah 46:10 (NASB)*

When God created, there was no human present to see that amazing event, but during the times of the Gospels, Jesus acted, and His miraculous power was seen by many. The water became wine, the dead rose to life, the leper was healed, the storm immediately calmed, the two fish fed thousands, the blind saw, demons obeyed, the lame walked, and so forth. (John 2:1-12; Mark 1:29-42; 2:8-12; 4:35- 41; Mark 5:38-42; Mark 6:34-44). Wouldn't it have been quite thrilling to have seen the power of the universe go forth and immediately change death to life, sickness to health, need to plenty, a raging storm to calmness, and many more miracles?

God's power and love

God's power and love are a trustable and reassuring combination. Many leaders throughout history have done awful and quite horrifying things because they have the power to do them. Think of Hitler. Human power can be driven by self-interest, recklessness, or worse. However, God's power is always driven by His love. The reality about the One True God is this - He is all-powerful and can do whatever He wants, yet, out of love He willingly held back His all-powerful nature to suffer and die on the cross for us (Romans 5:8; 1 Corinthians 1:18). Do you feel safe with God since His power is driven by His love? I certainly do!

> *Once God has spoken; twice I have heard this: that power belongs to God; and lovingkindness is Yours, O Lord...*
> *Psalm 62:11-12 (NASB)*

God's power is absolute

Many people just do not understand the infinite power the One True God has. There are movies, books and popular TV shows that portray the One True God's power as limited. If the hero or villain of the story is endowed with a so-called dark or light force, a magical box, or some spell or curse, then this person or group can manipulate God. If they knew about God from His Book, they would know how foolish their storylines really are. There is no force on this earth or in the universe, human or demonic, that has any power over God (Isaiah 40:10-26).

Our power

No one in history except Jesus has been all-powerful. Some people would like to be all-powerful, but thank God they are not. Power does seem to corrupt sooner or later. God certainly won't make us all-powerful, but He has given us power in Jesus (Ephesians 1:18-20). We receive Jesus' power through the Holy Spirit coming to live within us when we believe in Him (Acts 1:8). God wants us to have access to the power we need to live the right way, which is His way, and we have that power through Him (Philippians 4:13; Colossians 1:29).

> *...but the people who know their God will display strength and take action. Daniel 11:32b (NASB)*

God's power in creation

I think many of you could quickly share an example of the power of God from creation. The example that comes to my mind is when we lived in the mountains. Since our elevation was close to 8,000 feet, the lightning bolts would strike in an extremely powerful way right by our house - you could feel their energy. It was very scary. Every time those storms would hit, they would make me realize God's immeasurable power.

The storms of life can be most frightening, but you need to remember your all-powerful God is with you. Go to Him in prayer. He will give you the power to overcome. (Ephesians 3:20; Philippians 4:6-7).

~Life Application~

The power of God saves Daniel

<u>Daniel chapter six</u> is the popular Bible story of Daniel in the lions' den. Because of God's absolute power over everything, God easily kept Daniel safe from the mouths of many hungry lions all night. *Read Daniel 6:10-27.*

Describe God's power from Daniel chapter six.

Why did Daniel trust in God to protect him? Would you have?

Explain an example of God's power in creation.

How does God being all-powerful help you?

I have noticed, when I am willing to acknowledge God and ask for His power; I abundantly receive His power to overcome anything, and my feeling of powerlessness is replaced by His peace and confidence (John 16:33; Romans 15:13; Ephesians 3:20).

Exhortation: Rely on God's power more and more, and He will help you rise above whatever is stopping you from reaching His best.

God is Eternal, the Source of Life
~Day Eight~

The One True God is eternal

Since the One True God is the Creator and the LORD, I AM, the Self-Existent One, of course He would be eternal, timeless, everlasting, and without beginning or end.

> *Before the mountains were born, or You gave birth to the earth and the world, even from everlasting to everlasting, You are God. / Remember the former things long past, for I am God, and there is no other; I am God, and there is no one like Me, declaring the end from the beginning... Psalm 90:2; Isaiah 46:9-10 (NASB)*

The Source of Life

Jesus Christ is the source of all life, and without Him there would be no life. Furthermore all things continue to exist because of Him (Hebrews 1:3). It's pretty obvious we wouldn't have life if God hadn't given us life. Even many people who don't believe that God is the Creator recognize something or someone gave us life. As Christians we just happen to know Who that Someone is.

> *All things came into being through Him (Jesus)... In Him was life, and the life was the Light of men. / Jesus said to him, "I am the way, and the truth, and the life; no one comes to the Father but through Me." / ...in Him all things hold together. John 1:3-4, 14:6; Colossians 1:17 (NASB)*

Eternal life

It is clear God created Adam and Eve, as well as all of us, to have eternal life, but sin happened. In Genesis 2:16-17, God gave Adam and Eve just one command that they needed to obey or lose eternal life. They were not to eat fruit from one tree in the garden that was full of other lovely fruit trees. As you know, they chose to eat from the tree that God had told them not to. A world-wide nuclear war would have had less life-changing effects on all of us. Their disobedience against God brought sin into the world, followed by death. Humankind went from eternal life to death (Romans 5:12).

However, God wasn't going to allow the people He loved to remain in a state of eternal death, away from Him. So Jesus, the source of all life, took on death for us, so we could again have eternal life instead of eternal death. The key to gaining eternal life is belief in the One Who is the source of all life (Colossians 1:15-17).

Did you know we are created to be eternal? I think a lot of people believe that when we die, we just decay, or we become a part of some cosmic force in the universe. However, the Old and New Testaments teach something different. They teach death is a temporary separation of our soul and spirit from the body, not extinction of self; in the future, our soul and spirit will be reunited with our bodies (1 Corinthians 15:42-44, 49; James 2:26a). After we die physically, we are either with God in heaven or away from Him. Both existences are eternal. (Psalm 16:9-11; Matthew 22:31-32 also Exodus 3:15; 2 Thessalonians 1:8-10).

The compassion of Jesus Christ brings us life

The story of Jesus raising Lazarus from the dead in John chapter eleven, is one of the most unbelievable but true stories in the Bible. This Bible passage shows us so clearly that God is the source of life. It also gives us a dynamic view of God's power - Jesus spoke and brought immediate life from death. John 11:17-45 is summarized below:

> *So when Jesus came, He found that he (Lazarus) had already been in the tomb four days... Martha then said to Jesus, "Lord, if You had been here, my brother would not have died. Even now I know that whatever You ask of God, God will give You." Jesus said to her, "Your brother will rise again." Martha said to Him, "I know that he will rise again in the resurrection on the last day." Jesus said to her, "I am the resurrection and the life; he who believes in Me will live even if he dies, and everyone who lives and believes in Me will never die. Do you believe this?" She said to Him, "Yes, Lord; I have believed that You are the Christ, the Son of God..." Therefore, when Mary came where Jesus was, she saw Him, and fell at His feet, saying to Him, "Lord, if You had been here, my brother would not have died." When Jesus therefore saw her weeping, and the Jews who came with her also weeping, He was deeply moved in spirit and was troubled, and said, "Where have you laid him?" They said to Him, "Lord, come and see." Jesus wept. So the Jews were saying, "See how He loved him!" But some of them said, "Could not this man, who opened the eyes of the blind man, have kept this man also from dying?" So Jesus, again being deeply moved within, came to the tomb. Now it was a cave, and a stone was lying against it. Jesus said, "Remove the stone." Martha, the sister of the deceased, said to Him, "Lord, by this time there will be a stench, for he has been dead four days." Jesus said to her, "Did I not say to you that if you believe, you will see the glory of God?" So they removed the stone.*

Then Jesus raised His eyes, and said, "Father, I thank You that You have heard Me. I knew that You always hear Me; but because of the people standing around I said it, so that they may believe that You sent Me." When He had said these things, He cried out with a loud voice, "Lazarus, come forth." The man who had died came forth, bound hand and foot with wrappings, and his face was wrapped around with a cloth. Jesus said to them, "Unbind him, and let him go." Therefore many of the Jews who came to Mary, and saw what He had done, believed in Him. John 11:17-45 (NASB)

As you see, this story also shows a beautiful picture of God's compassionate love for us, by His weeping over the people's suffering from the consequences of death. Remember, God doesn't like it when we suffer, and He certainly didn't want us to die. Why would anyone not want to believe in this God?

I have always loved this story about Jesus. It magnificently shows Jesus being our source of life through His life giving power, as well as gives us a wondrous view of His compassion for us. What are your thoughts about this story?

~Life Application~

Our resurrection

Read John 11:17-45 again from your Bible if you have time. Reflecting on John 11:17-45, describe Jesus from this passage.

First Corinthians chapter fifteen describes what Jesus Christ gave to us through His death and resurrection – the hope of eternal life with a heavenly resurrected body. Remember, Jesus said in John 11:25-26, *"I am the resurrection and the life; he who believes in Me will live even if he dies, and everyone who lives and believes in Me will never die."* Read 1 Corinthians 15:3-4, 20-23, 42-44, 49-58.

Describe a Christian's future from these verses.

What are your thoughts on being an eternal being?

The rapture of Christians. 1 Corinthians 15:51-52 and 1 Thessalonians 4:13-18 describe the rapture. I am sure some of you are thinking, "What in the heck is the rapture?" It is when Jesus Christ will descend from heaven with a shout. This will cause the dead (also called asleep) in Christ to immediately rise with their new resurrected bodies. After that the Christians who are alive will rise too; and then all of us will meet together with Jesus in the clouds. Exciting!

There are different views on when in the future the rapture will take place; but when it does, it will surely be a supernatural happening that will affect the world.

What are your thoughts on the rapture?

Exhortation: Your part in eternal life is simply to believe in the source of life, Jesus. Then the guarantee and hope of the resurrection will be your future.

Week Three

Days Nine through Thirteen

~Notes~

God is Sovereign Over All
~Day Nine~

The One True God is sovereign

God is the supreme ruler of the universe. He is the King of kings and the Lord of lords who reigns eternally. Only God has the freedom and power to absolutely do what He wants; so as our loving King, His desire was to fight to the death to save us. (1 Timothy 1:17). Compassionate sovereignty, isn't it?

As you know from history, kings and rulers come and go; but the One True God's sovereignty will never cease. There is no human or demonic force that can control or defeat God. There is no military force, nor any weaponry, even from our high tech world, that will ever destroy or conquer God and His kingdom. Revelation, chronologically the last book of the Bible, ends with God and His kingdom in absolute dominance over the magnificent New Heavens and Earth that God had just re-created (Revelation 21:1-5). This should give us all unwavering hope and anticipation, because as Christians we are in God's everlasting kingdom (2 Timothy 4:18; 2 Peter 1:11).

> *...O Lord... are You not God in the heavens? And are You not ruler over all the kingdoms of the nations? Power and might are in Your hand so that no one can stand against You. 2 Chronicles 20:6 (NASB)*

We all have battles throughout our lives. Some of the battles are very brutal, such as relational betrayal, health problems, or perhaps real military battles. These battles can easily make you fearful, anxious, or worse. But we need to remember, God is our conquering and victorious King, Who is with us through it all (Deuteronomy 20:1-4). My son was in many battles in Iraq, and would tell you God was there with him. Do you allow God to fight your battles with you?

Our loving Sovereign God

As you will see by reading Isaiah 40:10-28, God is the sovereign ruler over the whole universe. He created all things and easily controls them. The most powerful world leader is nothing compared to the One True God, as King Nebuchadnezzar in Daniel chapter four would say. However, God always rules with compassion and care. Isaiah 40:10-28 is summarized below:

> *Behold, the Lord GOD will come with might, with His arm ruling for Him... Like a shepherd He will tend His flock, in His arm He will gather the lambs, and carry them in His bosom; He will gently lead the nursing ewes. Who has measured the waters in the hollow of His hand, and marked off the heavens by the span, and calculated the dust of the earth by the measure, and weighed the mountains in a balance, and the hills in a pair of scales? Who has directed the Spirit of the LORD, or as His counselor has informed Him? With whom did He consult and who gave Him understanding? And who taught Him in the path of justice and taught Him knowledge, and informed Him of the way of understanding? Behold, the nations are like a drop from a bucket, and are regarded as a speck of dust on*

the scales; behold, He lifts up the islands like fine dust... All the nations are as nothing before Him, they are regarded by Him as less than nothing and meaningless. To whom then will you liken God? Or what likeness will you compare with Him... It is He Who sits above the circle of the earth, and its inhabitants are like grasshoppers, Who stretches out the heavens like a curtain and spreads them out like a tent to dwell in. He it is Who reduces rulers to nothing, Who makes the judges of the earth meaningless... But He merely blows on them, and they wither... "To whom then will you liken Me, that I would be his equal?" says the Holy One. Lift up your eyes on high, and see Who has created these stars, the One Who leads forth their host by number, He calls them all by name; because of the greatness of His might and the strength of His power, not one of them is missing. Why do you say, O Jacob, and assert, O Israel, "My way is hidden from the LORD, and the justice due me escapes the notice of my God"? Do you not know? Have you not heard? The Everlasting God, the LORD, the Creator of the ends of the earth, does not become weary or tired. His understanding is inscrutable... Isaiah 40:10-28 (NASB)

As you saw in Isaiah chapter forty, God is the supreme ruler of all creation, yet He governs by love (Ephesians 2:4-7, 5:2). The conquering emperor of France, Napoleon Bonaparte, in the early 1800s at the end of his life, stated that he and Alexander the Great founded huge empires by military brutality and force; but Jesus Christ founded His kingdom upon love.

THE LORD your God is in your midst, a victorious warrior. He will exult over you with joy, He will be quiet in His love, He will rejoice over you with shouts of joy. Zephaniah 3:17 (NASB)

Our God is the sovereign ruler of the universe Who carries you lovingly in His arms (Isaiah 40:11). He rejoices over you. How do you feel about that?

Our free will and God's sovereignty

God is sovereign so why do we have free will? We could say, God in His sovereignty created us to have a free will, and He allows us to use it. God also gave us a free will so we can freely choose whether to love and obey Him or not. Sadly, Adam and Eve chose to use God's gift of free will to disobey Him. Do you?

~Life Application~

What does God's sovereignty mean to us

Read Isaiah 40:10-28 again in your Bible, if you have time. Describe God's sovereignty from this passage.

Our Sovereign God gives us a wonderful promise in Isaiah 40:29-31. *Read Isaiah 40:29-31.*

<u>Trusting in God.</u> Since God is in absolute control of all things, and always governs by love - we can trust Him.

You might be wondering what *trust* means? Faith and belief both mean being firmly convinced or completely sure about someone or something, which leads you to trust in that person or thing. When we believe in Jesus Christ, we trust Him to forgive our sins, giving us eternal life. From then on, we just don't wait around for heaven, we start living a life of trust in God. (Proverbs 3:5-6; Hebrews 11:1, 6).

Trusting boils down to who or what you choose to rely on, depend upon, or have confidence in. Who do you normally rely on? Is it God, or someone or something else? It's a moment by moment decision. (Jeremiah 17:5-8)

I had a colon cancer scare after a colonoscopy. Fear started taking control of me. Since I trust (have confidence) that God loves me, I started asking Him to control my fearful thoughts, give me His supernatural peace, and to speak to me through His Word. Bible verses such as Romans 8:28 started coming into my mind, and I realized after a day I did have His peace about the possibility of having cancer.

Exhortation: Depend on your King
Who is on His throne -
controlling all things for you through His love.

The One True God - His Characteristics and Names
50

The One True God is Holy
~Day Ten~

Perfect holiness

God is holy. This means He is completely separated from sin and evil; He is absolutely pure. He is the standard of holy. Since holiness comes from God, we cannot be holy without being associated with Him. God's holiness cannot tolerate sin, which means He can do no less than punish it. Holiness also has the idea of - to set apart, to sanctify, a separation from sin, as well as devotion to God and purity.[1] (Leviticus 20:26; 1 Samuel 2:2; Psalm 5:4; Isaiah 40:25).

> *...I the LORD ...am holy. Leviticus 21:8 (NASB)*

God's holiness and our sin

God's Word teaches us that we all are sinners just like Adam and Eve. This is because we are born with a nature that sins. (Psalm 51:3-5; Romans 3:9-18, 23, 5:12-19). It is reasonable to think that it is unfair that what Adam and Eve did thousands of years ago affects us today. The sad truth is, we all would have eaten from that tree.

Do some people sin worse than others? Of course, some people's sins add up to pure evil. Just read the news. Think of history. However, James 2:10 tells us, even if we were capable of sinning only once in our lifetime, we would still fall short of God's perfect holiness. I figure, I sin more than once a day because my thoughts and actions are not always holy. Yes, we all sin.

Our sin clearly presented a problem for God. He loved us and wanted to be with us, but He cannot tolerate sin since He is holy. Sad but true, our sin separates us from God.

> Behold, the LORD's hand is not so short, that it cannot save; nor is His ear so dull, that it cannot hear. But your iniquities have made a separation between you and your God, and your sins have hidden His face from you so that He does not hear. Isaiah 59:1-2 (NASB)

God's absolute holiness can have nothing to do with sin. In the Old Testament, if a person got near God's holy presence with intentional sin, in some cases that person would die (Leviticus 10:1-3). Even Israel's leader, Moses, who God said in Numbers chapter twelve was faithful in all God's household, didn't escape punishment because of his sin. In Numbers chapter twenty, God told Moses that since, as the people's leader, he didn't treat Him as holy by angrily disobeying God's instruction, he would not live to go into the land that God promised (Deuteronomy 32:48-52).

What does God's holiness mean to you? Does it make you afraid? It makes me afraid, and it should.

In the Old Testament times, people could have "a holiness" if they dedicated themselves to God; this meant setting themselves apart to God and abstaining from impurity.[1] But people still struggled with sin, so they were always falling short of God's perfect holy standard. It was obvious something needed to be done about sin and God did it.

Holiness in Jesus

Jesus Christ solved the problem of our sin and God's holiness. Jesus, Who is perfectly holy and hates sin with His whole being, willingly took our sins upon Himself when He died on the cross. This allows all who believe in Jesus to be set free from the power of sin and reconciled to God, making them holy (sanctified), with the outcome of eternal life. When we are sanctified or made holy, this is called sanctification.[1] (Mark 1:24; Romans 6:22-23; 2 Timothy 1:9).

> *...through Him to reconcile all things to Himself, having made peace through the blood of His cross... And although you were formerly alienated and hostile in mind, engaged in evil deeds, yet He has now reconciled you in His fleshly body through death, in order to present you before Him holy and blameless and beyond reproach... / ...but you were sanctified, but you were justified in the name of the Lord Jesus Christ and in the Spirit of our God. / ... To Him (Jesus) who loves us and released us from our sins by His blood... Colossians 1:20-22; 1 Corinthians 6:11; Revelation 1:5 (NASB)*

Jesus' death set you apart from sin, so you can have His holiness - making you holy. What are your thoughts on Jesus dying to make you holy?

~Life Application~

Our holiness as Christians

As Christians, our position is one of holiness in Jesus Christ. However, as we live our lives as Christians, we still need to intentionally practice holiness and not sin. This is because our sin nature is still with us on this earth tempting us to sin.

You might be wondering what holiness should look like in our lives? It's a devotion to the One True God, with a commitment to follow His Word. It's also sharing in God's purity; with a determination to abstain from sin, even though we could never be sinless as God is.[1] *Read 2 Corinthians 1:12; Ephesians 1:3-4, 4:20-24, 1 Peter 1:14-16.*

Our sanctification (holiness) in Jesus has three parts to it:[2]

1. Because of Jesus Christ and His Spirit coming to live within us - we are sanctified (set apart) from sin (made holy) at the moment of our salvation. (1 Corinthians 6:11; Colossians 1:19-22).

2. As Christians, we experience the process of sanctification which we can call "growing in holiness." This is where the Holy Spirit, with our cooperation, slowly but surely throughout our lives, transforms us into the image of Jesus. (Romans 6:19, 8:6-8; 2 Corinthians 3:18; 1 Thessalonians 4:7-8).

3. In heaven our sin nature will be gone. We will be completely set apart from our sins - living in perfect holiness. (1 Thessalonians 5:23; Jude 24-25).

Do you think you have been cooperating with the Holy Spirit in growing in holiness?

Reflecting on what holiness looks like for me: It's remembering I am only holy because my holy God took my sin upon Himself. It's recognizing my holiness comes from the Holy Spirit within me, so I need to be letting Him lead me. It's intentionally obeying God's Word, which allows me to live out holiness. It's wanting to please my holy God - not our sinful world, or my sinful self. What does holiness look like in your life?

Exhortation: God's abiding holiness is living within you, let it lead you into devotion to Him.

The One True God is Righteous and Just
~Day Eleven~

Perfect righteousness and justice

God's righteousness and justice are always acted out perfectly. God is righteous; He does exactly what is right. There is no lawlessness in Him. He is the final standard of what is right. God is just; He is perfectly fair. His justice has no bias in it. God's justice rewards righteousness and punishes sin. We could say, God's holiness is His essence, and righteousness is His way by which His holiness is expressed.[1]

> For I proclaim the name of the LORD ... His work is perfect, for all His ways are just; a God of faithfulness and without injustice, righteous and upright is He. Deuteronomy 32:3-4 (NASB)

Sin and punishment

I am sure you realize disobeying laws no matter where you live, always comes with a negative consequence. I can get in a hurry in my car, so of course I have gotten speeding tickets from breaking our city's speed laws. As a result, I am punished with a fine. Sin has punishment, because it is disobeying God's laws. Death and eternal punishment away from God are the punishment for sin. (There are two forms of death in the Bible: Spiritual death which is separation from God, and physical death.[2])

For the wages of sin is death, but the free gift of God is eternal life in Christ Jesus our Lord. Romans 6:23 (NASB)

Righteousness in Jesus

God never wanted to punish us. The Bible says that God told Adam and Eve *not* to eat the fruit from the tree of the knowledge of good and evil. He did not want them, or us, to die! He created us to be with Him, not to be dead to Him. However, since justice and righteousness are His characteristics, He has to fairly and rightly deal with all disobedience. If He did not, He wouldn't be just or righteous. Remember, He rewards righteousness because He is just. However, because He is just, He will punish unrighteousness which is sin.

Nevertheless, you can't catch God off guard. He had a plan set in eternity to deal with our sin, so He wouldn't have to punish us. That incredible loving plan was for Jesus to pay for the destructive consequences of our sins, taking the punishment we deserved upon Himself (Isaiah 53:5-6). This allowed us as Christians - to be justified (declared righteous), to have God's just anger against our sins satisfied, and to be completely forgiven of those sins. (1 Corinthians 1:30, 6:11; 2 Timothy 1:9; 1 Peter 2:24). When God looks at us, He doesn't see our sin, but instead He sees Jesus Christ's righteousness.[1] Loving justice, isn't it?

But God demonstrates His own love toward us, in that while we were yet sinners, Christ died for us. Much more then, having now been justified by His blood, we shall be saved from the wrath of God through Him. For if while we were enemies we were reconciled to God through the death

of His Son, much more, having been reconciled, we shall be
saved by His life. / He made Him who knew no sin to be
sin on our behalf, that we might become the righteousness
of God in Him. Romans 5:8-10; 2 Corinthians 5:21
(NASB)

We could say, having Jesus' righteousness allows us to go from God's enemy to His friend. How do you feel about Jesus taking your sins upon Himself and giving you His righteousness?

When Christians sin

Should we care about sin (unrighteousness) in our lives, since Jesus took our punishment for our sins? Of course! When we sin as Christians, we are still disobeying God's laws, which He put in place to give us well-being on this earth.

Sin is never good for us! Frankly it can devastate our lives if we habitually continue in some sins. I read this story the other day, and realized it gave an analogy of how sin can harmfully infect our whole being (Psalm 32:3-5, 38:3-5, 18). Sadly, a man contracted an infection that caused his body tissues to die, resulting in his untimely death. The dying of his tissues made his body give off a smell so foul, people would instinctively want to stay away from him. Sin is like a foul garment of death on us, spiritually sickening us, which God doesn't want to be near. (Isaiah 59:2; Isaiah 64:6-7; Romans 6:23a). Sobering analogy!

In regard to our sin problem as Christians - when we confess our sins or agree with God about our sins, it gets the foul garment of sin off of us, cleansing our unrighteousness and restoring our closeness to God again. Confessing your sins is the easiest way God could give you to be quickly near Him again (Psalm 32:1-5). When you sin, God knows it, whether you think so or not. Confess it and move on with Him.

> *If we confess our sins, He is faithful and righteous to forgive us our sins and to cleanse us from all unrighteousness. 1 John 1:9 (NASB)*

God's Word, the guide to righteousness

As Christians, God wants us to live righteously in Him. At times we think we are doing righteous acts but we are not (Isaiah 64:6). God's Word teaches you what is right to do, and what isn't - so you need to know His Word. I was just thinking, a number of people around the world can't afford a Bible or can't read one if they had one. They would love to have God's Word accessible. Those of us with a Bible are blessed, so let's intentionally be using it to learn the fundamentals of God's righteousness. This will give you the knowledge you need to live righteously, and not sinfully. (Psalm 1; 2 Timothy 3:15-17).

~Life Application~

Growing in God's righteousness

As you just learned, we have Jesus' righteousness living within us as Christians. However, we still need to be purposefully growing in righteousness. Psalm 23:3 says that God wants to guide you in the paths of righteousness. Ask God to help you live a just and righteous life. It is a prayer I pray for myself and my family just about every day. *Read Psalm 37:5-6; Matthew 6:33; Romans 3:22, 6:16-19, 14:17.*

Write down your insights from these passages on righteousness.

Ephesians 4:22-24 uses a clever illustration about how to grow in righteousness. [3] The original language of the New Testament was Greek. So from a few Greek words in these verses - you are being told to lay aside or put off that old foul garment that represents your old sinful nature, and to put on your new garment of righteousness (Job 29:14; Isaiah 61:10; Zechariah 3:3-5).[3] What these verses are simply saying is: Christians need to put off or stop the sins in their lives, and instead put on or do what Jesus would do. You will see examples of these "put off sins to put on what is right" in Ephesians 4:20-5:2. *Read Ephesians 4:20-5:2.*

Make a list from Ephesians 4:20-5:2 on what you should or shouldn't be doing. Then go do what is right.

Do you want to be found wearing a stinky old coat of sin that doesn't fit you any more, or a beautiful new coat made just for you in righteousness and holiness by your God? You do have a choice.

Exhortation: Live victoriously in Jesus' righteousness
by seeking what He wants you to be doing.
Do not seek the world's ways.

The One True God is Merciful
~Day Twelve~

The mercy of God

God is merciful. This means He feels great compassion and heartfelt sympathy towards us because of our suffering and struggles - the misery from sin. His mercy gives Him an active desire to remove those miseries from us. God's mercy also brings alleviation of the consequences of our sin. God loved us in mercy and gave to us in grace, resulting in our eternal life with a rich inheritance in heaven. (2 Corinthians 1:3-4; 1 Peter 1:3-5). When you think no one has sympathy or compassion towards you, remember God does! He died to give you compassion.[1]

> *The LORD longs to be gracious to you, and therefore He waits on high to have compassion on you... Isaiah 30:18a (NASB)*

God's mercy is shown to us through Jesus Christ

We didn't deserve God's mercy, because we were walking on a path of rebellion against God. There was no reason for God to show us mercy, because as sinners we were His enemies, deserving His wrath. We didn't love God but He loved us, and sent His Son to die for us, so we could receive His mercy. (Romans 5:9-10; 1 John 4:10). God's mercy towards me, makes me want to lift up my hands toward the heavens in thanksgiving, and say to my God, "I love you, LORD!" Is God worth your love? He thinks you are worth His love.

And you were dead...in your sins, in which you formerly walked according to the course of this world...Among them we too all formerly lived in the lusts of our flesh, indulging the desires of the flesh and of the mind, and were by nature children of wrath... But God, being rich in mercy, because of His great love with which He loved us, even when we were dead in our transgressions, made us alive together with Christ (by grace you have been saved). Ephesians 2:1-5 (NASB)

The life-changing power of God's mercy

About 24 years ago in Rwanda, a man wielding a machete killed a woman's child, and cut off her hand while doing it. Years later, this same woman decided to give mercy to the man that killed her child, and as a result she forgave him. Now they are friends serving the God that gave them both mercy and forgiveness through the death of His Son.

When I first read the story above, I thought, "How can the woman have mercy on the man who killed her child?" Then God made it very clear to me - it was Him and His loving mercy within her. God's mercy, as the story illustrates, works miracles in our lives.

But when the kindness of God our Savior and His love for mankind appeared, He saved us, not on the basis of deeds which we have done in righteousness, but according to His mercy...whom He poured out upon us richly through Jesus Christ our Savior. / ...keep yourselves in the love of God, waiting anxiously for the mercy of our Lord Jesus Christ to eternal life. Titus 3:4-6, Jude 1:21 (NASB)

Giving others mercy always seems to bring about a beautiful relational healing. I have seen it many times in my life and in others. We all need mercy. I know I need it quite often. You too?

Our merciful High Priest

High Priest is a name of Jesus. In the Old Testament, God appointed priests to offer sacrifices, prayers and praise to Him on behalf of the people. In doing so they made the people acceptable to come into God's presence in a limited way. The head priest was called the high priest.

Things changed in a very wonderful way in the New Testament. Jesus became our eternal and merciful High Priest. Instead of offering animal sacrifices, Jesus offered Himself once, to permanently pay for our sins. Because of Jesus' sacrificial mercy on the cross, we can now be in God's very presence, and pray and praise Him personally.

Our High Priest, Who is on His throne in heaven, is always with us. He always intercedes for us. He can sympathize with us because He has been one of us. He will always give us His abundant grace and mercy. (Romans 8:34; Hebrews 4:14-16, 7:23-27). As I write this, even after decades of knowing God, I am still in awe over how much the One True God does for us because He loves us.

How do you feel about your High Priest's compassion toward you?

~Life Application~

A question of mercy

<u>John chapter eight</u> is about a woman caught in adultery. *Read John 8:1-11.* Would you have picked up a stone and thrown it at her? The punishment for adultery was stoning. Or would you have given her mercy? Jesus gave her mercy. Jesus was probably writing the sins of everyone around Him in the sand, to remind them that they are sinners too. We need to keep in mind we are sinners, needing mercy and forgiveness. This thought helps me to give mercy to others. How about you?

None of us deserves God's mercy, but He abundantly gives us sympathy and compassion. We want mercy but at times refuse to give it to others. Ask yourself, do you show other people mercy? If you are having trouble showing mercy, just remember the rich mercy God has given you, even when you don't deserve it. *Read Matthew 5:7; Luke 6:35-36; Hebrews 4:14-16.*

From these passages write down some insights about mercy.

Exhortation: Ask for God's mercy.
It will always be there waiting
to give you the compassion you need.

"For the mountains may be removed and the hills may shake, But My lovingkindness will not be removed from you, And My covenant of peace will not be shaken," says the Lord who has compassion on you.   Isaiah 54:10

The One True God - His Characteristics and Names

The One True God is Good and Does Good
~Day Thirteen~

The Creator of goodness

The Bible tells us God is good, and what He does is good. God is the source of all goodness. There is no evil or bad in God; He is Holy (Psalm 5:4). We can see God's goodness in creation and our lives. In Genesis chapter one it says God created the world very good for us. There is a song that talks about giving the person's lover the stars and moon if he could. Well, God can and did. Out of love for us, the Creator literally gave us the stars and moon, the flowers and trees, and so on - so we could live with goodness all around us. Loving gift, isn't it?

You (God) are good and do good... Psalm 119:68 (NASB)

When life is going good, it seems a natural fit for us. There is a serenity in our hearts, isn't there? This is because we were made for an existence that was completely good. Good in the Bible is defined by the words - beautiful, delightful, happiness, pleasant, glad, precious, correct, excellent, lovely, convenient, joyful, fruitful, secure, kind, and righteous.[1]

Did you realize that every good thing comes from God? The colorful sunrise that I saw yesterday was from God. The pleasant odor after the rain came from God's sagebrush. When someone loves you, that love came from God, because He created love. The goodness that is all around us is from God. Without God there would be no goodness.

Do not be deceived... Every good thing given and every
perfect gift is from above, coming down from the Father of
lights, with whom there is no variation or shifting shadow.
James 1:16-17 (NASB)

When evil entered our world

God had created everything very good and wanted it to stay
that way. However, through the first sin, evil along with
death entered the world (Genesis 3:1-13). We were created
to only possess life and good, but the caustic effects of evil
took hold because of sin. Our world went from a place
where well-being, peace and joy naturally flourished - to a
place where struggling, suffering, sickness, and conflicts
thrived. Even though evil permeates our world, because of
His mercy, God causes good to flourish (Psalm 27:13-14,
34:8-10, 85:10-13).

Evil (or bad) in the Bible is defined as - inferior, wicked, evil,
malignant, hurtful, injurious, pain, unhappiness, misfortune,
adversity, calamity, unpleasantness, immoral, hideous, and
fierce.[2] Have you ever thought about how very different
things would be without evil in the world?

To be honest, I find it hard to imagine the world without
evil. I am looking forward to going back to an environment
that is only good in heaven.

God's goodness overcame evil in this world

Since God allows things that are difficult and even devastating, we can doubt whether He really is good. In fact trusting that God is good can be quite impossible from a human perspective at times. A friend of mine's daughter was killed. She struggles at times whether God is really good. I know God understands her struggle because He knows all things. I know He isn't thinking, "How dare she not think of Me as good." God is compassionate. He understands our struggles from evil. He weeps for us because of our suffering from evil and death (John 11:35). God literally gave His life to overcome evil.

Trials from an eternal perspective

All suffering needs to be looked at from God's perspective, an eternal perspective. He knows what trials need to happen to us for the best eternal outcome for us. Frankly, I have wondered if some of the worst situations on this earth will turn out to be the most beautiful when we see the results of them in heaven. Trials also can make us into being more like Jesus. It is always good to be more like Jesus, isn't it? (Romans 5:1-5; 8:18; 2 Corinthians 3:18; Philippians 3:20-21; James 1:2-5). The Apostle Paul who suffered a lot said,

> *For momentary, light affliction is producing for us an eternal weight of glory far beyond all comparison, while we look not at the things which are seen, but at the things which are not seen; for the things which are seen are temporal, but the things which are not seen are eternal.*
> *2 Corinthians 4:17-18 (NASB)*

God works all things for good

Because of Who God is, He will work even horrible things for our good and others. A good example of God working terrible trials for good, is the story of Joseph in Genesis. In short, Joseph's brothers had sold him into slavery out of jealousy when he was a teenager, and were hoping this treacherous deed would end in his death. Now it was many years later and Joseph (who is now second to only Pharaoh of Egypt) said to his brothers,

> *And as for you, you meant evil against me, but God meant it for good in order to bring about this present result, to preserve many people alive. Genesis 50:20 (NASB)*

We can trust God even when the going gets rough, because His good is being worked out in His plans for us (Romans 8:28). Trusting God leads to peace and strength when the world is in turmoil (John 16:33).

> *"For I know the plans that I have for you," declares the LORD, "plans for welfare and not for calamity to give you a future and a hope." / God is not a man, that He should lie... Has He said, and will He not do it? Or has He spoken, and will He not make it good? Jeremiah 29:11; Numbers 23:19 (NASB)*

What a wonderful promise that God works all things together for our welfare!

God feels bad about our suffering

Here's an illustration from my life to hopefully give you a little understanding of how God feels when suffering hits. My second son during his toddler years cut his head three times. Each ordeal of stitches turned out to be so traumatic for him - I felt awful. It was so hard for me to see my child in such pain and distress. I can still recall how distressed I felt, each time the doctor put him in a straight jacket to put the stitches in.

If I felt awful when my son was suffering, how do you think God feels when you and I suffer? He is so much more loving and caring than I am. We are His children. In reality, we love and care because we are created in His image. God also sees suffering from eternity, and we don't. I believe nothing happens to us that God won't use in a beneficial way in the present, in our future and into our eternity. (Romans 8:18; 1 Peter 1:3-7). Have you ever thought maybe God feels worse than you do about your struggles and suffering? (Exodus 3:7-9; Isaiah 63:9; John 11:33-38). Remember, He died to stop suffering.

~Life Application~

God's goodness triumphs

If you don't feel God is good, ask Him to show you His goodness in your life. I do when I am struggling with God's goodness. He always answers my heartfelt struggles. We also need to remind ourselves, God is using the trials and tribulations of life for our good, to make us more like Him, whether we feel it or not. *Read Psalm 23:4-6; Jeremiah 33:2-3; Romans 5:1-5, 8:28; Philippians 4:5b-7; James 1:2-5.*

What are your thoughts from these passages?

My son was in Iraq as a Marine officer. He saw many upsetting and destructive things, but he also saw God's goodness. I have found in our world that is full of evil, I need to intentionally look for the good around me, and be thankful for it.

Prayerfully look for the good in your life, and make a list of those good things. Then thank God for them.

Exhortation: The Creator of goodness -
wants you to rely on Him
to work His good in all things.

Week Four

Days Fourteen through Seventeen

~Notes~

God Gives Grace, He is Gracious and Patient
~Day Fourteen~

The grace of God

The One True God always showers us with His grace (or favor). "Grace upon grace" in John chapter one means that because of Jesus, God's favor will continually be upon us. Is there anyone in your life who would favor you constantly? Probably not, because as life is, we all mess up more than we want to think, and people aren't gracious and patient like God is. Isn't it an amazing gift that we are in God's continuous favor throughout our lives and into eternity?

> *...and we saw His glory, glory as of the only begotten from the Father, full of grace and truth... of His fullness we have all received, and grace upon grace... grace and truth were realized through Jesus Christ. John 1:14, 16-17 (NASB)*

Late one night while at home, my husband and I heard a loud noise that sounded like a car crash. God put it on our hearts to get into our car and go see if anyone needed help. As we turned onto the road we saw flames. When we got there, I ran to the car on fire and pulled the driver out, because his door was miraculously open. The others in the car were dead. My husband helped the people in the other car. The driver didn't deserve favor because, being drunk, he caused the accident that killed his two friends and hurt the passengers in the other car. As sinners we are wrecks before God, not deserving His favor either, but still God gives us His grace upon grace.

Grace defined

Grace is a beautiful word with a beautiful meaning. Grace has the idea of favor, beauty, joy, acceptance, benefit, pleasure, gratitude, and kindness in it. A gracious thing, act, or person brings kindness, thankfulness, joy, and beauty to the receiver. Grace goes beyond what is expected from the giver, and has no expectation of something in return. In other words, grace is favor freely given to you - you don't earn it. In human terms grace/favor is only given to a friend, not to an enemy.[1]

However, God's grace goes beyond human grace. Even though we were God's enemies because of our sin, He still loved us and rejoiced over us, so He wanted to freely shower His grace upon us. Do you feel your sins can never be forgiven? God's grace forgave you (Romans 3:23-24, 5:15, 21; Ephesians 1:7). Are you struggling with life? His grace is sufficient for your every need or struggle (2 Corinthians 9:8). Do you feel helpless or perhaps overwhelmed? God's grace will give you the power you need to overcome anything (2 Timothy 1:9, 2:1). Have you lost a loved one, or maybe are afraid of death? The grace of God gives you absolute assurance of eternal life (Ephesians 2:4-9).[1]

How do you feel about God's favor towards you? It amazes me about every day.

Salvation, a gift of grace from Jesus

Because of the awful fix we were in as sinners, it's pretty evident salvation had to be given to us by grace, so God freely gives us His unearned and undeserved favor, bringing salvation to us (Romans 11:6). We receive the gracious gift of being saved from our sins like we would receive any gift - we take it. However, instead of using our hand to take the gracious gift of salvation from God, we take it by belief or faith in Jesus Christ.[1] This is an amazing truth which is almost too good to be true, but it is.

> *But God ... because of His great love with which He loved us, even when we were dead in our transgressions, made us alive together with Christ (by grace you have been saved) ...so that in the ages to come He might show the surpassing riches of His grace in kindness toward us in Christ Jesus. For by grace you have been saved through faith; and that not of yourselves, it is the gift of God; not as a result of works, so that no one may boast. Ephesians 2:4-9 (NASB)*

God is patient and slow to anger

I was over at my friend's house, when her husband put his fist through the wall because he was angry at her. It was a scary situation. Since we can have a tendency to not do what God wants us to do, we would be in an awful fix if God wasn't extremely patient with us and slow to anger. Remember, God has every right to be angry at us because of our sin. Yet, because of His great love for us, He died to satisfy His just wrath against each and every sin. (Isaiah 54:7-8; Micah 7:18-19; Romans 5:8-9). I am very relieved God is slow to anger, and patiently waits for me to do what I should be doing. Are you?

> *...But You are a God of forgiveness, gracious and compassionate, slow to anger and abounding in lovingkindness; and You did not forsake them. / The Lord...is patient toward you, not wishing for any to perish but for all to come to repentance.* Nehemiah 9:17; 2 Peter 3:9 (NASB)

Because God is Who He is, He wishes no one to perish eternally, so He is patient with all people, wanting all to choose to believe in Him. I don't know about you, but I do not patiently wait very easily for anything. To think the God of the universe patiently waits for us, so we can have a happily ever after future with Him, touches my heart. Have you chosen to believe in Jesus (John 3:16)? He is patiently waiting for you.

Grace along with patience

Grace and patience certainly go together. If you want to show someone grace, you must show them patience too, or you are not being very gracious to them.

The One True God shows grace and patience to us, to lovingly encourage us to do what is right. The Old Testament prophet Jonah hated the wicked Assyrians (whose capital was Nineveh) and knew God would be slow to anger and abundant with His grace towards them. So Jonah ran from God to try to stop God from being patient and gracious to the Assyrians. But God can't be fooled, and He sent a big fish Jonah's way. This fish showed Jonah God's grace and patience, by saving him and getting him back on God's track. And Jonah was right, because God did show the very sinful Assyrians much patience and grace through Jonah's preaching, which led them to repent. (Jonah 1:1-3, 15-17, 2:10, 3:1-10, 4:1-2). There is amazing grace and patience for us too from our God!

~Life Application~

The amazing power of God's grace

Amazing Grace is a popular song even with people who don't know the One True God, because we all love grace. The writer of the song, *Amazing Grace,* was a slave trader at one time, who found God's grace. That grace changed him from a man who abused people, to a man who loved God and people. *Read Romans 5:21, 11:6; 1 Corinthians 15:10; 2 Corinthians 9:8; Ephesians 1:7-8, 3:7; 2 Timothy 1:9.*

What has God's grace done for you personally?

God's grace has given me an assured hope for eternal life, as well as a confidence and contentment in my life that I thought would never be possible.

Grace or bitterness? (Hebrews 12:15). If you are not willing to give people grace and patience, bitterness can grow in your life and cause a lot of problems. Bitterness is deep seated ill feeling or hostility towards someone. Think about a person who has no grace or patience. He is not very pleasant to be around, is he? Are you a bitter person? If so, it's time to change. Ask God to make you a patient and grace giving person. You will like the new you and everyone else will too. (Matthew 7:12; 2 Corinthians 1:12; Ephesians 4:1-3, 30-32).

Share a few thoughts on being a patient and gracious person.

Exhortation: When others are unkind, even mean,
remember the grace of God is upon you,
to hug you in His constant favor and kindness. Rest in Him.

The One True God is Unchanging
~Day Fifteen~

God doesn't change

God is unchangeable or immutable. This means He is always the same. Since God never changes, His promises in His Word are assured to us. What God says is what will happen; He keeps His word. (Isaiah 55:10-11).

> *For I, the LORD, do not change... / ...He (God) is not a man that He should change His mind. Malachi 3:6a, 1 Samuel 15:29b (NASB)*

Do you sometimes feel your salvation isn't certain? Since God never changes, of course this means Jesus Christ's sacrifice will always take away your sins as He has promised it would (1 John 5:11-13). I am very grateful I can completely depend on God never changing His mind about me going to heaven. Are you?

> *Jesus Christ is the same yesterday and today and forever. Hebrews 13:8 (NASB)*

Trust in the unchanging nature of God

I know it is hard for us to understand someone who never changes. This is because we live in a world that seems to constantly change. Your husband liked the blue dress, so you bought it, then he changes his mind. Your boss tells you to do some research, and then gets frustrated you spent time on it. Your son joined the military, so your house seems empty. The ladies in your support group suggest that you tell your sister to stop calling you, so you do, and then they tell you that is unloving. You need to move to a different state, so there go multiple changes. Even church leaders can say one thing and end up doing another. I don't know about you, but it certainly is hard on me to navigate through a world that is almost completely governed by whims of change.

I am so glad our God never changes; He is our rock. We can trust in Him. (Isaiah 26:3-4). Is God your rock?

God's love is unchanging

God is unchanging, so His love for you will never change. Have you ever loved someone but they were unfaithful to you? God's love is faithful love. He loved you before the world was created. He loved you when you were His enemy. He will love you throughout eternity. (Jeremiah 31:3; Ephesians 1:4). Do you love Him? He loves you.

> *Who is a God like You...He delights in unchanging love.*
> *Micah 7:18 (NASB)*

What does it mean to you that God's love is unchanging towards you?

Does God change His mind

God doesn't change His mind, but that doesn't mean He is inflexible. God's anger burned over Israel's awful sin, but God listened to Moses and changed His mind over destroying them (Exodus 32:7-14; Jonah 3:10). Does this mean God changes His mind? No! God is eternal and sovereign over all, yet He responds to an individual's needs, attitudes and actions in the present.[1] God knows all things, so of course He would respond to Moses with exactly what was right. We could say, God is never unloving and deals with every situation through Who He is, not just through His unchanging nature. (Psalm 106:43-46; Romans 8:31-39).

~Life Application~

The same yesterday and today and forever God

Describe a situation that has frustrated you about change in the world in general or of someone who has changed.

Why would God's unchanging nature give you peace in that frustration?

I am involved in politics, which definitely makes me feel nothing stays the same. In politics, sometimes the change is very good, other times not so good. I find myself quite often thinking this or that situation looks like it is out of control, leading to a devastating state of affairs, but then I remember our all-powerful, all-knowing, all-wise, gracious, patient and merciful God is in control (Jeremiah 29:11). God's unchanging nature gives me peace of mind for the future, no matter who is governing our country (John 16:33).

Exhortation: You can place your hope
in God, because He won't change
His mind about His promises.

The One True God is Faithful
~Day Sixteen~

Perfect faithfulness

God will always remain faithful. This means what He says, He does. He keeps His promises and is absolutely trustworthy. God died to keep His promise of eternal life. God's Word shows His faithfulness through promises spoken and kept. In actuality, because of Who God is, He can only be faithful.

> *God is faithful, through whom you were called into fellowship with His Son, Jesus Christ our Lord. / If we are faithless, He (God) remains faithful, for He cannot deny Himself. / For the word of the Lord is upright, and all His work is done in faithfulness. 1 Corinthians 1:9; 2 Timothy 2:13; Psalm 33:4 (NASB)*

The importance of faithfulness

God knows how important it is to our psychological health to be able to trust, to have people around us who are faithful. This makes sense because we were created to trust, and to trust God (Psalm 22:9-10; Proverbs 3:5-6). How do you feel when someone promises to do something but doesn't do it? If people are untrustworthy, it causes stress and uncertainty in our lives. When people keep their promises, life has a security and certainty to it, and is much easier to handle. God always keeps His promises; He is faithful so you can trust in Him.

...Has He said, and will He not do it? Or has He spoken, and will He not make it good? Numbers 23:19b (NASB)

Our ultimate trust should be in God

We have all trusted in people that ended up being unfaithful to us, one way or another. In reality, putting our ultimate trust in people who are imperfect isn't the best idea. All of us are capable of letting each other down. I know I am.

It's God Who is always faithful, that's where our ultimate trust and hope should be. Jeremiah 17:5-8 paints a true to life picture of how beneficial trusting in God is, compared to trusting in people. Trust God and thrive, or trust in people, and struggle. You have a choice.

> *Thus says the LORD, "Cursed is the man who trusts in mankind and makes flesh his strength, and whose heart turns away from the LORD. For he will be like a bush in the desert, and will not see when prosperity comes, but will live in stony wastes in the wilderness, a land of salt without inhabitant. Blessed is the man who trusts in the LORD, and whose trust is the LORD. For he will be like a tree planted by the water, that extends its roots by a stream and will not fear when the heat comes; but its leaves will be green, and it will not be anxious in a year of drought, nor cease to yield fruit." Jeremiah 17:5-8 (NASB)*

I live in the desert so I can easily envision Jeremiah 17:5-8. In our yard the trees have lavish green leaves and seasonal blooming (that give us all allergies) because they get plenty of water. However, the trees in the surrounding desert wilderness struggle.

Trustworthiness of salvation

We can depend on the trustworthy statement that Jesus
Christ came to save us from our sins. Remember, He died to
keep that promise.

> *It is a trustworthy statement, deserving full acceptance,*
> *that Christ Jesus came into the world to save sinners,*
> *among whom I am foremost of all. 1 Timothy 1:15 (NASB)*

Are you glad you can trust in God to forgive your sins?
(Acts 10:43).

Are you faithful

I just heard a story about a heroic dog that fits with
faithfulness: It was night. A family's house was in flames.
The family dog saved the whole family from dying by going
to each room and barking to wake them. Sadly the dog died
saving his family. (What a strong example of God's
faithfulness seen in His creation.) I think I can safely say,
this dog understood faithfulness better than some people do.

How to be faithful? A faithful person is one who does what
she says she will do. She keeps her promises. She is
intensely loyal, sincerely honest and not hypocritical. She is
someone people can trust. As Christians we are faithful to
God by doing what He wants us to do, in other words, by
following His Word. If you are not a faithful and
trustworthy person, you need to be. Ask the Holy Spirit to
keep you faithful.   (Galatians 5:22-23).

~Life Application~

Faithfulness in action

Daniel chapter three is about a golden image and three
godly men who refused to bow down to it. Since these three
men wouldn't worship the image, King Nebuchadnezzar
had them thrown into a fiery furnace. They were saved
from this fiery death by our faithful God, Who was in the
furnace with them. *Read Daniel 3:4-7, 11-30.*

Describe God from this passage.

To be honest, I don't know if I could have trusted God like
Shadrach, Meshach and Abed-nego did (Daniel 3:28). But
that's how trust in God works; you wholly trust in Him,
empowering you to do the humanly impossible. Could you
have trusted in God's faithfulness like Shadrach, Meshach
and Abed-nego did?

Whether you feel God is with you or not, He is; because He
is faithful. He will never forsake you. (Isaiah 49:14-16).
Remember, when you are going through a trial, the One
True God is walking with you, no matter how difficult it
gets. Have you felt God's faithful presence through a trial?

How do you feel about God's faithfulness? Does it give you strength in a trial? Does it make you feel secure in Him? Does it give you hope for the future? Does it give you confidence in His Word and in your prayers?

Understanding God's faithfulness gives me the confidence I need to teach God's Word, and yes, publish this book. It makes me know He is with me, even if I don't feel He is. When I pray, I can trust He will always answer; whether I like His response or not, I know His answer is what I need.

Exhortation: Trust in Jesus. He will faithfully walk with you through life, even the fires of life, and bring you safely into heaven.

God is Truth, He is Truthful
~Day Seventeen~

Perfect truth

The One True God is the God of truth. There is no falsehood or lie found in Him. He is the living and true God. His Spirit is also called the Spirit of truth. God defines what is true in His Word, and that truth gives us knowledge of Him and the way to life.

> *And we know that the Son of God has come, and has given us understanding so that we may know Him who is true; and we are in Him who is true, in His Son Jesus Christ. This is the true God and eternal life. / ...you turned to God from idols to serve a living and true God. 1 John 5:20; 1 Thessalonians 1:9b (NASB)*

Jesus says to us in John 14:6, that He is the way, the truth and the life. Only in Jesus are we guaranteed the truth of life for now and eternity. Do you pray to the living and true God? If you want the truth, He is the One to go to.

We need truth

When I was getting my Masters in Social Work, we would have discussions on what truth is. Many students felt it was okay to make up their own truth. I personally thought this was an illogical view. For instance, if you have cancer, would you want the real truth, or a made up truth about your treatment options? The truth always sets me free from confusion; it always leads me in the right direction. I think we would agree, we need truth to navigate through life.

Truth or consequences

We need to be truthful with people. A person told me that a woman in our church thought I was being very unfriendly to her. So I went to the woman to apologize. She laughed and said, "Don't believe anything that person says." When someone lies, people start to not believe anything the person says. If you are in the habit of lying, you are affecting your relationships in negative ways. (Proverbs 12:17-20, 19:9). We need to be truthful, so people can trust us. Aren't you relieved God is always truthful, so you can trust Him?

> *God is not a man, that He should lie... Numbers 23:19a (NASB)*

God's Word is truth

> *So Jesus was saying... "If you continue in My word...you will know the truth, and the truth will make you free." John 8:31-32 (NASB)*

God's Word is the absolute truth because it was God Who inspired each author to write what He wanted (2 Timothy 3:16a; 2 Peter 1:20-21). I believe we have all had doubts about God's Word being completely true. I know I have. God doesn't mind our doubts if we let our doubts lead us to a deeper understanding of Him and His Word.

I don't have the room here to discuss in-depth the intellectual reasons of why the Bible is the true Word of God, but let's quickly look at some evidence that shows its authenticity. The Bible has more manuscript evidence to support its authenticity than any ten pieces of classical literature combined. The Jews preserved the Old Testament writings like no other manuscript; each word, syllable and letter was counted for accuracy. No book was put in the New Testament except the books which were written by one of Jesus' twelve Apostles, or by a close associate of theirs (Acts 2:42; Ephesians 2:19-20).[1]

God's truth is seen through fulfilled prophecy from the Bible. Fulfilled prophecy has always made me think that only Someone Who truly knew the beginning to the end of time could have known these events to write about them. The Old Testament contains nearly 300 references to the coming Messiah (Savior). Jesus Christ fulfilled them all. Many other prophecies from the Bible have already been fulfilled concerning the nation of Israel, the rise and fall of nations and kings, and so on.[1]

I always like to know the intellectual reasons of why something is true. But when it comes to the things of God, you must also combine Who God is into the equation. Therefore, why wouldn't God simply throughout history keep His Word absolutely true for the people He loves, so that we can know Him and His plans for us?

> *For as the rain and the snow come down from heaven, and do not return there without watering the earth and making it bear and sprout ... So will My word be which goes forth from My mouth; it will not return to Me empty, without accomplishing what I desire, and without succeeding in the matter for which I sent it. Isaiah 55:10-11 (NASB)*

God's Word is God's will

God's Word is the truth that allows us to accomplish God's will. If you want to do God's will, then do what His Word says. I know there are gray areas that God doesn't completely enlighten us on in the Bible, but everything God wants us to know about Him and His will is revealed to us through His Word. Yes, God does use other things to show us who He is (such as His creation), or to give us clarity about His will, but these other things should *never* contradict His Word. Ask the Spirit to create in you a desire to make His Word the primary guiding influence in your life. (Psalm 119:105; Colossians 1:9-12).

> *Be diligent to present yourself approved to God as a*
> *workman who does not need to be ashamed, accurately*
> *handling the word of truth. 2 Timothy 2:15 (NASB)*

What are your conclusions about God's Word?

~Life Application~

The truth about your afterlife

I believe everyone searches sooner or later for the truth about their afterlife. I did a lot sooner than most people, probably because my mother died when I was 5 years old. The afterlife is one theme I have studied quite a bit in the Bible. And believe me, I am very thankful I can depend on God's truth about eternity. When God says I will have eternal life through belief in Jesus Christ, I know for sure I will. Not having the truth about the path to heaven can make your future hell.

The truth that gives us eternal life: *Read Matthew 1:18-25; John 3:14-18, 14:1-9, 1 Corinthians 15:3-4, 2 Corinthians 5:19, 21; Ephesians 2:4-9.*

Summarize from these passages on why you can have eternal life.

*Exhortation: Listen to the living
and true God - He will guide
you in truth.*

As the deer pants for the water brooks, So my soul pants for You, O God.
My soul thirsts for God, for the living God... Psalm 42:1-2a

The One True God - His Characteristics and Names

Week Five

Days Eighteen through Twenty-One

~Notes~

The One True God is All-Knowing
~Day Eighteen~

God is omniscient

Omniscient means God knows all things. I have some geniuses in my family. They know a lot, but there are many things they know nothing about. God knows everything. His knowledge is endless, ceaseless, and timeless. In Genesis chapter one, God spoke and His spoken intelligence formed everything we know, and many things we do not understand yet (Psalm 33:6-9).

> *...For the LORD is a God of knowledge... / Therefore do not go on passing judgment before the time, but wait until the Lord comes who will both bring to light the things hidden in the darkness and disclose the motives of men's hearts...*
> *1 Samuel 2:3; 1 Corinthians 4:5 (NASB)*

God is the "know it all" of the universe

There is nothing God doesn't know about His creation: He knows when lightening zips across the evening sky, rain touches the earth, and where the rivers should run. He knows when the wild goat climbs the mountain cliffs, and the salmon swims upstream. He knows when a duckling breaks out of its egg, a little bird falls out of the sky, and of course He knows everything else. (Psalm 104:1-30). His knowledge and power also keep all of creation, including us, existing and thriving (Colossians 1:17).

God knows everything about you and me: God knew of you before He created the universe (Ephesians 1:4). He knows your every thought, feeling, intent and motive. He knows what you need before you do. God knows when you are struggling even though you have told no one. God knows when you have sinned even in your thoughts. He knows when you are loved or unloved, treated well or badly, or accused rightly or wrongly. God knows it all, and wants to counsel, protect and strengthen you. (Psalm 16:7-11, 32:5-8, 91:1-4).

> *O LORD, You have searched me and known me. You know when I sit down and when I rise up; You understand my thought from afar. You scrutinize my path and my lying down, and are intimately acquainted with all my ways. Even before there is a word on my tongue, behold, O LORD, You know it all. You have enclosed me behind and before, and laid Your hand upon me. Such knowledge is too wonderful for me; It is too high, I cannot attain to it.*
> *Psalm 139:1-6 (NASB)*

When my grandmother was a child, she was at home alone one day. As she was walking to her bedroom she felt a gentle but firm hand on her shoulder. She looked around but no one was there. It scared her, so she ran outside to get a neighbor. Throughout my grandmother's life she would say, God's loving hand stopped her and saved her life, because God knew a man with a knife was in her bedroom. He was an escaped prisoner.

Do you ask God for His counsel? Since He knows all things, it is the smart thing to do.

God's knowledge and our knowledge

God created us with a brain that naturally learns. Our mind is made to gain knowledge as we go through life, which means God definitely wants us to know and understand Him and the world around us. He gave us the intelligence we needed - to invent the wheel, create musical instruments, cure many diseases, invent computers, travel in space, produce abundant food supplies, and devise every good idea and invention throughout the history of our world.

We need God's knowledge. Human knowledge has its limitations because of such things as intelligence, competence, experience, education, and social impact. The harmful effects of sin on both our physical and psychological functioning also affect our knowledge capabilities. I think it is a no brainer (yes a pun), we need God's unlimited knowledge. So it just makes sense, if you want God's knowledge, then you must know Him and ask Him for understanding. (Daniel 1:17, 2:20-23; Romans 11:33; 1 Corinthians 2:16).

> *Ask, and it will be given to you; seek, and you will find; knock, and it will be opened to you. For everyone who asks receives, and he who seeks finds, and to him who knocks it will be opened. Or what man is there among you who, when his son asks for a loaf, will give him a stone? Or if he asks for a fish, he will not give him a snake, will he? If you then, being evil, know how to give good gifts to your children, how much more will your Father who is in heaven give what is good to those who ask Him! Matthew 7:7-11 (NASB)*

God's Word teaches His knowledge

God has given us His Word and His Spirit to teach us His knowledge and wisdom (Psalm 119:130; John 14:26; 2 Peter 1:20-21). My friend and I have been reading through God's Word for years. We meet every few weeks to discuss what we have read. It makes for a wonderful friendship. Take the time and learn God's knowledge through His Word; you won't regret it.

> *All Scripture is inspired by God and profitable for teaching, for reproof, for correction, for training in righteousness; so that the man of God may be adequate, equipped for every good work. / Now we have received, not the spirit of the world, but the Spirit who is from God, so that we may know the things freely given to us by God.*
> *2 Timothy 3:16-17; 1 Corinthians 2:12 (NASB)*

~Life Application~

The all-knowing God is the all-loving God

Do you feel at times no one really knows the real you? Do you find yourself thinking, "If people really knew me they would hate me"? Well, God knows everything about you. He even knows the number of hairs on your head, and all your words before they come out of your mouth. (Psalm 139:1-6; Luke 12:6-7). Yes, God knows it all, and loves you no matter what. Does it reassure you to know God knows everything about you (the good and bad), and still loves you?

Read the book of Jonah. This is one of my grandson's favorite Bible stories, because he loves to fish, so of course he likes big fish. The story of Jonah is a quick read and has marvelous examples of God's characteristics in it, especially the fact God knows everything, so Jonah couldn't escape from Him.

Describe God from the book of Jonah.

How does the fact God is all-knowing impact your life? It sure impacted Jonah's.

Jonah didn't know, but God knew that Jonah's preaching in the city of Nineveh (in present day Iraq), would bring about a rich history of the One True God to that area. By the second century, Christianity had spread to that area, and it is still alive to this day on the plains of Nineveh, even in spite of persecution. God is all-knowing, so it makes sense to seek Him for what you should be doing. If you are doing God's bidding, who knows what wonderful things you might be accomplishing for future generations.

Exhortation: When you don't know where to turn or what to do, turn to the God Who knows it all, and delights in counseling you.

God is Wisdom, He is Wise
~Day Nineteen~

Perfect wisdom

The One True God's wisdom is perfect. He always sees and chooses the best and highest goals, and uses the surest means to achieve them. God's judgments and decisions are absolutely right. God is wise because He perfectly uses His knowledge and understanding. God's wisdom allows Him to take His knowledge and bring about the best results through the best means in everything He has done, is doing, and will do throughout eternity. (Job 12:13). Wisdom comes from God, so all true wisdom is certainly found through and in Him.[1]

> *Oh, the depth of the riches both of the wisdom and knowledge of God! How unsearchable are His judgments and unfathomable His ways! Romans 11:33 (NASB)*

Jesus is God's wisdom

Jesus Christ alone embodies God's wisdom (Romans 16:27). God's wisdom knew the only way we can get to heaven is through Jesus. When some people hear the way to be saved and to go to heaven is to believe in Jesus, they think it is too simple minded, so it is foolishness to them. But God in His wisdom and love did what needed to be done to save us, and to make the means of salvation a simple message. Great human wisdom wasn't needed, but only belief in the One crucified.[1]

For the word of the cross is foolishness to those who are perishing, but to us who are being saved it is the power of God. For it is written, "I WILL DESTROY THE WISDOM OF THE WISE, AND THE CLEVERNESS OF THE CLEVER I WILL SET ASIDE." Where is the wise man?...Where is the debater of this age? Has not God made foolish the wisdom of the world? For since in the wisdom of God the world through its wisdom did not come to know God, God was well-pleased through the foolishness of the message preached to save those who believe. For indeed Jews ask for signs and Greeks search for wisdom; but we preach Christ crucified, to Jews a stumbling block and to Gentiles foolishness, but to those who are the called, both Jews and Greeks, Christ the power of God and the wisdom of God. Because the foolishness of God is wiser than men, and the weakness of God is stronger than men. 1 Corinthians 1:18-25 (NASB)

The only wise God and us

Human wisdom is nothing compared to God's perfect wisdom. Human wisdom is the ability to make sound judgments and choices based on our knowledge, understanding, and experience. It's a virtue that every leader should want and every person should seek. As you know, some people are a lot wiser than others. Years ago, a neighbor painted his house a bright purple that everyone in the neighborhood was either mad about or joked about. I asked the guy, "Why such a wild, unusual color?" He said, "I was unwise by allowing my 8 year old daughter to pick the color for our house. And then I didn't bother to try out that paint color before I gave it to the painters." God's infinite wisdom is always perfect; where at times human wisdom isn't very wise, and can be, should we say, unbelievably foolish, or irrational, or worse.

*Yet we do speak wisdom among those who are mature; a
wisdom, however, not of this age nor of the rulers of this
age, who are passing away; but we speak God's wisdom in
a mystery, the hidden wisdom which God predestined
before the ages to our glory; the wisdom which none of the
rulers of this age has understood; for if they had understood
it they would not have crucified the Lord of glory.*
1 Corinthians 2:6-8 (NASB)

Our wisdom

God's wisdom literally lives within you, wanting to give you
the knowledge, understanding, and yes, the experience you
need to act wisely as a Christian. Yet, our capacity to be
wise or have good judgment comes from a strong
relationship with our wise God - a relationship of intentional
trust and prayer, letting His Spirit lead and apply His Word
to our lives. (1 Corinthians 2:12-13).

*The law of the Lord is perfect, restoring the soul; the
testimony of the Lord is sure, making wise the simple.*
Psalm 19:7 (NASB)

God wants to give you His wisdom. He tells you to ask for
wisdom in James 1:5, and He will give it to you. Wouldn't
you rather have the wisdom of the ages (God's wisdom)
instead of man's limited wisdom? Do you ask God for
wisdom?

*...For wisdom and power belong to Him...He gives wisdom
to wise men, and knowledge to men of understanding.*
Daniel 2:20-21 (NASB)

God's wisdom and power

Because of God's immeasurable power and wisdom working together, the universe and earth are a perfect habitat for us and life (Psalm 104:24; Proverbs 3:19; Colossians 1:16-17).

My husband, Tom, who is a physicist says:

> *The sun, moon, and other heavenly bodies all follow their courses in perfect precision; atoms form molecules perfect for life; the earth is a perfect distance from the sun, and the sun is a perfect distance from the center of the Milky Way; light travels at exactly the right speed; even the strength of electric, magnetic, gravitational, and nuclear forces all have exactly the right values; if any of these things were different we could not exist on the earth. Scientists call this the anthropic principle,[2] and they have no explanation on why these things should be. However, those of us who know the Creator understand it was His power and wisdom that "fine tuned" our world and universe for us.[2]*

Since God can perfectly create life and keep it perfectly sustained, shouldn't you put your trust in God? Do you trust in God? It's the wise thing to do. (Daniel 6:23).

~Life Application~

Wisdom applied

These passages talk about what God wants you to do. *Read Colossians 1:9-12, 3:12-17; James 1:5.* Write down a few wise things you should be doing.

Mercy
Kindness
Humility
Gentleness
Patience
Forgiveness
Love
Live in Peace
Always be Thankful.

I pray, Lord, for complete knowledge of Your will, and for spiritual wisdom + understanding. Please strengthen me with your glorious power so I will have all the endurance + patience I need.

This passage compares two types of wisdom: God's beneficial wisdom to human wisdom that can bring disorder even evil. *Read James 3:13-17.* Summarize this passage.

*Exhortations: Let it be your goal to trust
in your wise God and follow His wise Word.
Don't let your well-being depend on the world's wisdom.*

The One True God is Always with You
~Day Twenty~

God is omnipresent

Omnipresent means God's presence is always there. In other words, there is nowhere you can go that God isn't with you. If you are up in space, or deep below the earth's surface, or in the remotest parts of the sea, or in the furthermost wilderness, God is there.

Yet, if it wasn't for Jesus making us holy by His death on the cross, God would always be there for us, but our ability to draw near to God would be very limited because of our sin. Jesus opened wide the door for us to have an intimate and eternal relationship with the One True God. (Colossians 1:19-22; Hebrews 10:19-22). If it wasn't for Jesus where would we be.

> Jesus said... "I am with you always, even to the end of the age." Matthew 28:20b (NASB)

God is with us

God is always with us ready to care and protect us. In 2018, God was with the 12 young boys and their soccer coach in the dark and flooded cave in Thailand for those many frightening days. God's loving hand miraculously led the rescue that united the world and saved those boys.

Growing up, I was alone a lot. When I was afraid I would call out to God, wanting Him there. Years later, when I read Psalm one hundred thirty-nine, I realized God was already with me even before I called to Him. Personal God, isn't He?

> *Where can I go from Your Spirit? Or where can I flee from Your presence? If I ascend to heaven, You are there; if I make my bed in Sheol, behold, You are there. If I take the wings of the dawn. If I dwell in the remotest part of the sea, even there Your hand will lead me, and Your right hand will lay hold of me. If I say, "Surely the darkness will overwhelm me, and the light around me will be night," even the darkness is not dark to You, and the night is as bright as the day. Darkness and light are alike to You. For You formed my inward parts; You wove me in my mother's womb. I will give thanks to You, for I am fearfully and wonderfully made; wonderful are Your works, and my soul knows it very well. My frame was not hidden from You, when I was made in secret, and skillfully wrought in the depths of the earth; Your eyes have seen my unformed substance; and in Your book were all written, the days that were ordained for me, when as yet there was not one of them. Psalm 139:7-16 (NASB)*

God's Word also tells us He formed us in our mother's womb. This means He was with you and me when we were just embryos. In other words, we have never been away from God's presence.

I get up early most days to seek God, pray and write; in that quietness I feel God's presence. Is there a special time or place you feel God is close to you?

God is there - call to Him

When you want to pull your hair out because life seems out of control - don't - because God is there wanting to get you through the chaos (Psalm 18:31-36). When you are not sure what to do, and you need understanding, wisdom and strength, turn to God; He is always there (Isaiah 40:27-31). When there is trouble and darkness seems all around, don't be afraid. The light of His presence is there.

I can find myself fretting about a cancer diagnosis, a difficult relationship, my children's well-being, a javelina eating my flowers, or whatever life brings my way, and forgetting that God is with me. Can you relate? We just need to remember that God is unquestionably with us, and for goodness sakes, we need to be deliberate in asking Him for help. Whether we feel God is there or not, He is. Call to Him! (Deuteronomy 20:1-4; Psalm 4:1, 18:6, 73:23-26).

Hide or seek with God

We can't hide from God. This makes sense because He is always with us. But how many times have you found yourself thinking, "I hope no one sees or hears that." I have certainly thought that. Are you trying to hide something from God? Well, you can't because He is always with you. Go to God even with your deepest secrets and sins. I do. He will give you grace and lovingly help you. (Psalm 32:7-8; Romans 8:31-37; 1 Corinthians 4:5).

"Am I a God who is near," declares the LORD, *"And not a God far off? Can a man hide himself in hiding places, so I do not see him?" declares the* LORD. *"Do I not fill the heavens and the earth?" declares the* LORD. *Jeremiah 23:23-24 (NASB)*

~*Life Application*~

Look for God, He is there

A young friend of mine had a sister die in a car accident. I went over to her house to see how she was doing. She took me into her sister's bedroom and told me to look at the closet door mirrors that were about 6 feet across. There on the mirrors were written in big letters, "God is with me. I will be with Him in eternity." I said, "That's neat, you wrote that?" She said, "No! My sister wrote it just before she got in her car to drive to work." We both cried. God knew her sister would be with Him within the hour. So God put it on her sister's heart to write those sentences that meant a lot to her; and at the same time God would use it to let her family know in a very concrete way that He definitely was with their daughter/sister and will continually be. Incredible story, isn't it? God is always there, so be deliberate in seeking Him and calling to Him; He will be found (Psalm 91:15). And sometimes He will allow you to see Him in miraculous ways like in this story.

I love Psalm one hundred thirty-nine; it details how intimate God is with us. *Read Psalm 139.*

Write down your favorite insights related to God from this Psalm.

Exhortation: The best place to find true joy is in God's presence. Let His presence flood your mind by memorizing His words.

The One True God is All-Seeing and All-Hearing
~Day Twenty-One ~

God hears and sees it all

Since God is eternal, always present, all-knowing, and all-powerful, then of course He sees and hears everything. God sees and hears what is happening now, but He has also seen and heard everything in the past, and will in the future. God isn't like me, who unwisely closes my eyes while heading into the bushes on my bike. God's eyes are wide open, and He sees everything, and acts for our best.

> *And the Egyptians treated us harshly...and imposed hard labor on us. Then we cried to the LORD, the God of our fathers, and the LORD heard our voice and saw our affliction and our toil and our oppression; and the LORD brought us out of Egypt with a mighty hand... Deuteronomy 26:6-8 (NASB)*

God answers

There are numerous stories in the Old Testament that describe how God sees and hears and answers. A favorite of mine is: The Assyrians, the world power at the time, were laying siege to a small defenseless country named Judah (in 701 BC) to destroy it. A prayer from the defenseless nation's king, Hezekiah, put in motion God miraculously defending Judah, and defeating the Assyrians without even an arrow being shot. (Isaiah 37:14-21, 33-38).

Do you go to God in prayer like King Hezekiah did? Keep in mind, He will answer your prayer, but in His perfect wisdom and timing.

Jesus supernaturally perceives everything

The first four books of the New Testament, the Gospels, tell the story of Jesus living on the earth. In the Gospels you see that Jesus was yes, a person like you and me, but He was so much more, because He is God. Jesus supernaturally saw and heard everything around Him: The peoples' thoughts and motives, everyone's past and future. (Matthew 9:3-4; Luke 8:45-46, 11:17, 22:31-34; John 1:47-50).

A great example of Jesus supernaturally seeing and hearing everything around Him is in John chapter four: Jesus was sitting at a well of water, talking with a woman. The woman realized immediately Jesus was different. This is because He wasn't just talking to her kindly, but as they talked He could see and hear what the reality was behind her words. He knew exactly how she was living without her explaining. Jesus was seeing and hearing into her very heart and soul. This encounter with Jesus bought eternal life to the woman and many others. (John 4:7-19, 25-30, 39-42). How amazing it must have been to have communicated with the One True God face to face. Someday in eternity, we will too.

God sees our hearts

God looks at a person's heart; whereas we tend to look at the outward appearance of a person. As God told Samuel in the Old Testament,

> *Do not look at his appearance or at the height of his stature, because I have rejected him; for God sees not as man sees, for man looks at the outward appearance, but the LORD looks at the heart. 1 Samuel 16:7 (NASB)*

The heart generally means the mind. We could say, God sees and hears our thoughts, reasonings, understandings, will, desires, and motives. The inclination of our hearts and minds can be very evil, but our hearts and minds are transformed in beautiful ways through Jesus (Jeremiah 17:9-10; Hebrews 10:19-22). Isn't it a relief to know our hearts can be right before God and not guilty?

Have you ever thought you had godly motives but then God showed you otherwise (Psalm 7:9)? A man was helping his elderly neighbor with her yard, thinking he was just being kind. But then God showed him that He was really doing it so she would put him in her Will. We can lie to others, even to ourselves, but not to God. He sees our true motives, and then praises or convicts accordingly.

> *Therefore do not go on passing judgment before the time, but wait until the Lord comes who will both bring to light the things hidden in the darkness and disclose the motives of men's hearts; and then each man's praise will come to him from God. 1 Corinthians 4:5 (NASB)*

I definitely can have sinful thoughts and motives. Ask God to search your thoughts and motives for any sin (Proverbs 15:3). I do. If there is sin, confess it, and ask God to help you stop it. Remember, He will hear you (Psalm 32:5).

> *Search me, O God, and know my heart; try me and know my anxious thoughts; and see if there be any hurtful way in me, and lead me in the everlasting way. Psalm 139:23-24 (NASB)*

God watches over us

When I read this story years ago, I thought, "Wow, what a wonderful illustration of God watching over us." It was twelve days after the 2010 earthquake in Haiti, a man was miraculously found alive beneath the concrete and wood of a hotel grocery. He survived by diving under a table when the ceiling started to fall. He said, "It was God who heard my cry for help. He watched over me and was tucking me away in His arms. He gave me strength!"

> *The righteous cry, and the Lord hears and delivers them out of all their troubles. / For the ways of a man are before the eyes of the LORD, and He watches all his paths. / The eyes of the Lord are in every place, watching the evil and the good. / ...says God the LORD...I will also hold you by the hand and watch over you... Psalm 34:17; Proverbs 5:21, 15:3; Isaiah 42:5-6 (NASB)*

Maybe you are near death, as the man above was; possibly you are dealing with a difficult health problem; perhaps you are at work or a job interview; maybe you are celebrating your child's birthday or graduation; or simply on your daily walk - whatever your circumstance, bad or good, God is watching over you. Are you reassured and strengthened by this certainty?

~Life Application~

God compassionately hears and sees

God is called the God who sees and hears by a mistreated slave in Genesis chapter sixteen. Have you ever been mistreated by people who had authority over you? Well that's what happened to the slave Hagar. However, God saw and heard Hagar's affliction, protected her, and blessed her and her descendants. God told Hagar to name her son, Ishmael, which means God hears. The spring of water where she met God was named the well of the living One who sees. *Read Genesis 16:6-15.*

Describe God from Genesis 16:6-15.

How does knowing God sees and hears all things influence your life? It surely did Hagar's life.

God hears our every prayer like He heard Hagar's. Explain a recent prayer God answered in your life.

Yesterday morning on my walk, I asked God to help me set up a number of doctors' appointments. (If you have ever made appointments, you know it takes a lot of time, because invariably you get put on hold. It can be very frustrating.) That day in the mail, I received a schedule of all my husband's and my appointments which I wasn't expecting. Not really a miracle, but a huge blessing from God.

Exhortation: Sit with Jesus, and tell Him your fears and worries. He is listening, and has seen what has caused your distress.

Are not five sparrows sold for two cents? Yet not one of them is forgotten before God. Indeed, the very hairs of your head are all numbered. Do not fear; you are more valuable than many sparrows. Luke 12:6-7

The One True God - His Characteristics and Names

Week Six

Days Twenty-Two through Twenty-Six

~Notes~

The One True God is Incomprehensible
~Day Twenty-Two ~

The incomprehensibleness of God

God is incomprehensible. He is so much more incredible than our human reasoning could invent. God spoke and everything came into existence, and stays in existence because of Him. God inspired and His Word went forth to reveal Who He is. God determined and all of history unfolded. God loved and the world changed. God died and salvation came to all who wanted it. God empowered and miracles took place, and much more. How do you humanly explain these things? You can't! God's Word allows us to understand Who God is, but still His ways and thoughts are so wondrously above ours.

> *"For My thoughts are not your thoughts, nor are your ways My ways," declares the* Lord. *"For as the heavens are higher than the earth, so are My ways higher than your ways, and My thoughts than your thoughts." Isaiah 55:8-9 (NASB)*

Love beyond our understanding

God's love is incomprehensible to me. Before I was a Christian, I was God's enemy, enjoying the evil that made me His enemy. I didn't even know God, and surely didn't love Him, but He still wholeheartedly knew and loved me. It is hard for me to grasp completely why God loves me so absolutely and so unconditionally. How about you?

...and to know the love of Christ which surpasses knowledge, that you may be filled up to all the fullness of God. Ephesians 3:19 (NASB)

Miracle worker

The One True God is the miracle worker. Those of you who are familiar with the Bible, know it is full of God's beyond our understanding miracles. Here are a few of God's miracles in the Old Testament: A 90 year old woman, Sarah, had a son (Genesis 17:17, 21:2). God caused the Red Sea to unbelievably part so over a million people could escape the Egyptian army on dry land (Exodus 14:15-16, 19-22). As a teenager, King David trusts in God and kills a giant with one well aimed rock (1 Samuel 17:4-9, 32-37, 48-51). A prophet of God prays and a dead boy is raised to life (2 Kings 4:32-37).

Why incomprehensible

You are probably thinking, "I thought God wants me to know Him. How can I know Him if I can't comprehend Him?" Yes, God wants us to know Him, but with our present earthly limitations we simply can't *fully* comprehend Him. Realistically, we cannot understand anyone entirely, so bearing in mind Who the One True God is, it just makes sense we can't fully comprehend Him.

Sin also made God even more incomprehensible to us. When sin entered the world, we went from an existence of seeing God face to face to being separated from Him. Because of our sin, we were in spiritual darkness, so our ability to understand God and eternity became almost nonexistent.

But as you probably guessed, Jesus Christ solved the problem of our blindness to God. Only through Jesus and the enlightening of His Spirit do we receive the ability and desire to know God. In John chapter one, Jesus is called the true light that lights our way to God. (John 1:3-13, 3:16-21, 12:46, 16:13-15).

Still even as Christians, our earthly understanding dims in comparison to what our heavenly understanding will be (1 Corinthians 15:42-49). When we get to heaven, we will know God fully, as He knows us now. We will also see Him face to face. I can't wait! How about you?

> *For now we see in a mirror dimly, but then face to face; now I know in part, but then I will know fully just as I also have been fully known. 1 Corinthians 13:12 (NASB)*

The One True God and other gods

I think by now, you have come to realize how incredible the One True God is. His power is always driven by love, not self-centeredness like humans. His grace towards us extends into eternity. Even though God is the Self-Existent One who needs no one, yet He sacrificially loves us, pursues us and dies for us so we can be with Him.

No other faith has a deity like the God from the Jewish and Christian Scriptures. All other deities are elusive; their followers need to do prescribed works and rituals that never bring a certainty of righteousness, salvation or heaven. No other religion can claim a god like the Christian God, Who fervently pursues humankind to the point of death on a cross, so that we can be in an intimate relationship with Him, have His righteousness, and the certainty of a wondrous eternity with Him. (John 6:67-69, 14:1-3; Romans 3:22-26; 2 Corinthians 5:21; 1 John 5:20). Why would anyone not want to know and love this God?

> *To you it was shown that you might know that the LORD, He is God; there is no other besides Him... Know therefore today, and take it to your heart, that the LORD, He is God in heaven above and on the earth below; there is no other. Deuteronomy 4:35,39 (NASB)*

Our God is so vast and powerful, and needs nothing or no one to exist, yet He died so He could be with each and every one of us. Go to Him in prayer. He certainly loves to be with you - talking.

What are your thoughts on the One True God being incomprehensible?

~Life Application~

The incomprehensible God dwells with us

<u>In Mark chapter four,</u> Jesus performs a miracle to calm the sea and His disciples' fears. *Read Mark 4:35-41.* The last verse in this passage has His disciples stating, *"Who then is this that even the wind and sea obey Him?"* Yes, our God is beyond complete human understanding now, but when we get to heaven we will know Him fully. Wonderful truth, isn't it?

Describe Jesus Christ from this story.

How does this story speak to you?

Being afraid is a lack of faith!

Jesus asks, → "Why are you afraid? Do You still have no faith?"

Jesus, our Lord, will protect us!

Exhortation: The incomprehensible God dwells with you. Walk with Him. Talk with Him. Love Him. He is right there with you.

God is Kindness, He is kind
~Day Twenty-Three ~

Perfect kindness

The One True God is kind. His character illustrates kindness. Kindness is the character or disposition of a person that exemplifies good or goodness, does what is needed for a person, has a willingness to help, has no harshness but patience, gentleness, graciousness, and generosity. When someone's character is kind, that person naturally gives grace. A kind person is a loving and good-natured person.[1]

In the Gospels we see a dramatic living picture of the kindness of God being lived out in Jesus: He did what was needed to bring salvation; He was the embodiment of good, and acted in goodness; He was gentle and patient in His dealings; He generously provided, and gave grace upon grace.[1] (John 1:16-18, 5:5-9, 6:1-13, 10:7-11, 18:4-11, 19:25-30).

About every morning, I see the definition of kindness on my walk: A good-natured elderly couple gently guide their blind daughter as she walks with them. All three of them are gracious people, who say "hi" to everyone who passes. It makes my day. Do you enjoy kindness? I sure do!

God's kindness described

God's kindness purposely brought salvation to us. God couldn't be our God if His character wasn't utterly kind, as well as completely merciful, loving, gracious, patient and forgiving. As you can guess, if God's character was only one of holiness, justice, and righteousness, we would be helplessly bound to pay for our own sins in hell. Yet, because of Who our God is, He gladly took our punishment for our sin upon Himself. (Jonah 4:2; Hebrews 12:2). God's kindness and all His characteristics work together to give us salvation and a happily ever after future with Him. Compassionate God, isn't He?

> *But when the kindness of God our Savior and His love for mankind appeared, He saved us, not on the basis of deeds which we have done in righteousness, but according to His mercy, by the washing of regeneration and renewing by the Holy Spirit, whom He poured out upon us richly through Jesus Christ our Savior, so that being justified by His grace we would be made heirs according to the hope of eternal life. Titus 3:4-7 (NASB)*

Do you realize you and I deserved God's wrath, but instead He gave us His kindness? That makes me very determined to love and serve my God. What about you?

Eternal kindness is given to us through Christ Jesus. Human kindness seems to be a rarity in our world, but God's kindness never stops towards the world. Jesus lived out God's eternal kindness on this earth, which permitted Him to show us His grace in kindness throughout eternity. We are told in Ephesians 2:6-7, as Christians, we are seated with

Jesus on His throne in heaven (of course figuratively, but in reality that is how close Jesus is to us, and how certain heaven is), so that God can shower us with His grace in kindness in the ages to come.

> ... and raised us up with Him, and seated us with Him in the heavenly places in Christ Jesus, so that in the ages to come He might show the surpassing riches of His grace in kindness toward us in Christ Jesus. Ephesians 2:6-7 (NASB)

What does it mean to you that your eternity will be spent with God, and with Him being kind to you?

God's kindness brings repentance

Repentance involves a change of mind/heart towards God - a turning from sin to God - that leads to doing good instead of evil. Considering what we just learned about God's kindness towards us, of course His kindness should lead us to repentance. We could say, repentance is to change from a self-centered life to a God centered life.[2] God's kindness has saved me, and changed me for the good. How about you?

> Or do you think lightly of the riches of His kindness and tolerance and patience, not knowing that the kindness of God leads you to repentance? Romans 2:4

God's kindness and patience lovingly waited for us to change our minds about turning to Jesus, so we would not perish but have eternal life. God's kindness wishes no one to perish so He died to give us a choice.

The Lord is not slow about His promise, as some count slowness, but is patient toward you, not wishing for any to perish but for all to come to repentance. 2 Peter 3:9 (NASB)

~Life Application~

Living out God's Kindness

God gave us kindness when we didn't deserve it, and His kindness saved us. Let's work hard to show kindness to others. *Read Romans 2:4; 1 Corinthians 13:4; Galatians 5:22-23; Ephesians 2:4-7; Colossians 3:12; Titus 3:4-7.*

Describe God's kindness.

What do these passages say about kindness in our lives?

<u>Kind or angry?</u> There is a clear contrast in Ephesians 4:31-32 between mean reactions and kind reactions.

> *Let all bitterness and wrath and anger and clamor and slander be put away from you, along with all malice. Be kind to one another, tender-hearted, forgiving each other, just as God in Christ also has forgiven you. Ephesians 4:31-32 (NASB)*

The reactions in verse 31 lead to stress, discontentment and a person no one wants to be around.   The kind reactions in verse 32 lead to a gentle and good-natured person; who has contentment and compassion.

Ask yourself, what type of person do you want to be? The person God wants you to be, who brings kindness, love, and forgiveness into the world, or the mean, angry and bitter type of person? You have a choice.

Exhortation: When the cruelty of this world is pulling you down, go to God and His kindness will lift you up to comfort and support you.

The One True God is the God of Forgiveness
~Day Twenty-Four~

Perfect forgiveness

God gives us undeserved forgiveness. To forgive means to not keep account of wrongs, to send forth or away the wrong, and to let go from oneself. Forgiving also has the idea of treating the offending person graciously, with kindness, love. (1 Corinthians 13:5, Ephesians 4:32). God's forgiveness removes our sins from us; liberating us from sins' guilt and power. Only God can literally remove sins from a person, but you can still forgive or let go of the wrong against you from another person.[1]

> ...But You are a God of forgiveness, gracious and compassionate, slow to anger and abounding in lovingkindness; and You did not forsake them.
> Nehemiah 9:17 (NASB)

Forgiveness comes through Jesus Christ

We gain God's undeserved forgiveness through the death of Jesus. His sacrifice on the cross satisfied God's just anger over our sins, so that we could have our sins completely forgiven. God's forgiveness demonstrates to us His love instead of His wrath (Romans 5:8-10). Where would we be if God didn't forgive us?

To know Jesus is to know God's forgiveness. This is because God's forgiveness is only given to you through belief in Jesus.

> *...that through His name (Jesus) everyone who believes in Him receives forgiveness of sins. / In Him (Jesus) we have redemption through His blood, the forgiveness of our trespasses, according to the riches of His grace which He lavished on us.* *Acts 10:43; Ephesians 1:7 (NASB)*

God gave the ultimate sacrifice to forgive us - His Son. Would you sacrifice your son so a person could be forgiven? I would not, but God did. God sent His Son, Jesus Christ, to die on the cross for us. This act of love positively shows us God is determined to forgive us.

> *...If God is for us, who is against us? He who did not spare His own Son, but delivered Him over for us all, how will He not also with Him freely give us all things? Who will bring a charge against God's elect? God is the one who justifies; who is the one who condemns? Christ Jesus is He who died, yes, rather who was raised, who is at the right hand of God, who also intercedes for us. Who will separate us from the love of Christ? Will tribulation, or distress, or persecution, or famine, or nakedness, or peril, or sword? ...But in all these things we overwhelmingly conquer through Him who loved us. For I am convinced that neither death, nor life, nor angels, nor principalities, nor things present, nor things to come, nor powers, nor height, nor depth, nor any other created thing, will be able to separate us from the love of God, which is in Christ Jesus our Lord.* *Romans 8:31-39 (NASB)*

God's forgiveness takes away the guilty verdict and the eternal punishment that sin brings to us, and makes us righteous; and enables us to have a relationship with Him.

God's never-ending forgiveness

God's Word says our sins are completely removed from us when we believe in Jesus; they are remembered no more by Him. We could say, because of Jesus our sins are thrown into the depths of the sea never to be fished for again.

> ...Yes, You will cast all their sins, into the depths of the sea. / For I will be merciful to their iniquities, and I will remember their sins no more. / As far as the east is from the west, so far has He removed our transgressions from us. Micah 7:19b; Hebrews 8:12; Psalm 103:12 (NASB)

God also forgives us throughout our lives. In reality because of Jesus' payment for our sins, we live in God's forgiveness. When we sin as Christians, it does affect our relationship with God, but never our eternity. Our relationship with God can be immediately fixed by confessing our sin to Him (1 John 1:9). Your father, aunt, friend, and boss may not forgive you, maybe never, but God always will. When God says He will forgive you, you can believe Him, because He died to forgive you.

Forgiving others

Some people think if they forgive someone, they are saying that what the person did was acceptable. That is not what forgiveness means. When you forgive someone, you make the choice to give up your desire to get back at the person, and to let go of your anger towards the person. You also stop judging the person who caused you the hurt. Instead of revenge, anger, and judgment, you show grace and kindness. (Romans 12:17-21). In other words, the guilty person may not deserve forgiveness, but it's an act of kindness and love on your part to forgive (Ephesians 4:32). When you forgive, you are not condoning the person's sinful action, but you are letting it go from yourself. When you forgive someone, it doesn't mean the person won't experience the consequences from their behavior.[1]

A friend of mine in graduate school told me she grew up in a Christian family that was very unforgiving. In her teenage years her father and mother divorced. Then when she was in her forties, and near a divorce herself; she and her husband went to a marriage counselor. The counselor listened to both their perspectives on the marriage and then said, "The main problem in your marriage is both of you are conditional in forgiving the other." My friend said, "This comment shocked her, because she thought you should only forgive if the person deserved it." The counselor gave them a Bible study on forgiving. My friend told me the study changed her marriage, and her outlook on forgiving. When I met her, she was caring for her mother. My friend said to me, "My mother still isn't particularly patient and forgiving. Please pray for me to love and forgive my mom God's way." Can you relate to my friend's life?

How does knowing God is the God of forgiveness impact your life? It took away my feelings of guilt that I was raised under. God's forgiveness is healing, isn't it?

~Life Application~

Don't misunderstand forgiveness

How do you forgive? Do you forgive like God? Or does a person need to live up to your standards to be forgiven? If God didn't give us undeserved forgiveness, we would stay dead in our sins, because God's standard is perfect holiness (Isaiah 6:1-7). Remember, God forgave you when you were His enemy. God tells us to forgive others as He has forgiven us. *Read Psalm 86:5, 130:1-4; Luke 6:35-38, 11:1-4.*

Explain forgiveness from these passages

<u>On occasion do you feel God just can't forgive you?</u> When we feel this way, I believe what we are probably thinking is we can be right before God by our own good works. In other words, by doing what you think a good person should be doing such as telling the truth, being kind to your nasty neighbor and so on. God does like it when you do good; but the real problem is, you can never do enough good works to live up to God's perfect holy standard. This is because, to use a computer term, we have a nature that defaults to sin sooner or later. *Read Psalms 143:1-2; Matthew 5:48; Romans 3:9-18, 23; James 2:10.*

Jesus did something we could never do, He fulfilled God's perfect standard of holiness for us: He was born a Jew, which meant He lived under the Old Testament laws (good works) His entire life but never broke even one of them. He died for our disobedient acts toward God, not His own. In dying for our sins He fully paid off our debt to God from those sins. So let's not forget - we are forgiven because of Jesus and His sacrificial work, not from anything we have done, whether bad or good. *Read Isaiah 53:4-6; Romans 3:22-24, 8:1-2; Galatians 2:16; Ephesians 1:7; Colossians 2:13-14; 1 John 3:5.*

Why can you know you are forgiven by God?

Exhortation: Do not let sin weigh you down.
Ask God to forgive you, and He will.

The One True God is Love
~Day Twenty-Five~

Perfect love

In 1 John 4:8, the Bible says, "*God is love.*" This means that God's love is expressed in everything He does and says. God does not just love, He is love. God is sovereign, but His rule is acted out through His love. God is just, but every act of justice is done in His love. God is all-knowing, but His knowledge is guided by His love. Since God is love, He is always desirous to give us His merciful compassion. (Lamentations 3:21-23).

God's love in the New Testament

In the New Testament, the Greek word that best describes God's love is *agape/agapao*. *Agape* love springs from comprehending that the object of love is valuable. It highly values or esteems the one it loves, even if the one loved is unlovable. *Agape* is an act of the will (intentional, a conscious choice) that puts the welfare of the one loved above the one loving; it is not based on feelings or motivated by emotions. It's a compassionate act - selflessly giving of oneself to meet a need of another, even an enemy. It is also a love that compels the one loving to give by self-sacrifice for the good of the one loved. In other words, it is an unselfish, unconditional, and sacrificial love. Jesus' life models *agape* love.[1]

The most life-changing and sacrificial act of *agape* love is Jesus Christ dying for us. In John 15:13, Jesus says, there is no greater way of showing your love for someone than by dying for them. A mother in Russia gave her life so her daughter could live, by shielding her daughter from a suicide bombing. I feel we would all agree the mother showed *agape* love towards her daughter. Yet, even this mother's sacrificial love doesn't equal the *agape* love God has for us. Jesus had every right to receive our worship and our sacrifices, but instead the God Who created everything, Who is self-existent, sovereign, eternal, the source of all life, all-powerful, always present - allowed Himself to be sacrificed for us. (Revelation 1:5).

How do you feel about this? It makes me feel valued and loved.

> *In this is love, not that we loved God, but that He loved us and sent His Son to be the propitiation (offering) for our sins. 1 John 4:10 (NASB)*

I imagine people think God loves us out of duty, not out of desire. However, *agape* love suggests that the lover finds joy in the loved.[1] Hebrews 12:2 tells us Jesus found His joy in us so much that He endured the cross for us. Beautiful reality, isn't it?

> *… fixing our eyes on Jesus,…who for the joy set before Him endured the cross, despising the shame… Hebrews 12:2 (NASB)*

God's love in the Old Testament

In the Old Testament, the Hebrew word that best describes God's love is *hesed/chesedh*. This word is translated love, unfailing love, lovingkindness, kindness, favor, mercy, and loyalty. *Hesed* is not easily defined in a single word. The basic idea of *hesed* is - an act of love, kindness, mercy, or faithfulness shown towards someone you are in some type of relationship with. *Hesed* is a loyal, steadfast and faithful love. *Hesed* is the kind of love that would live out the wedding vows. In other words, it is a love that commits to the person and stays committed to them no matter what. God's *hesed* is a loyal love which is unfailing, everlasting, and intentional towards us.[2] (Isaiah 54:10).

The love of God

I was the wedding coordinator for a dear friend decades ago because I came free. I was standing with the bride just before she walked down the aisle, so I got to see firsthand her joy as she saw her groom. I also saw the groom's radiant face as he saw his beloved. What a beautiful moment in time. God's love makes me think of the joy and the total commitment a bride and groom have for each other on their wedding day. God loves to love you!

> *The Lord your God is in your midst, a victorious warrior.*
> *He will exult over you with joy, He will be quiet in His*
> *love, He will rejoice over you with shouts of joy.*
> *Zephaniah 3:17 (NASB)*

~Life Application~

Covenant of love

You are probably thinking, "What does the old-fashioned term covenant mean?" Simply put, covenant means a binding agreement with a person or people to whom you want or need to be in a relationship with for a purpose. Covenant in the Bible simply means, a binding relational agreement between God and His people in which God makes assured promises and expects certain behavior back.

There are many covenants in the Bible, but the everlasting covenant or new covenant is the central one. From past history blood seemed to be a part of some covenant making - to seal/confirm the covenant and show how binding it was. Our responsibility in the everlasting covenant is to believe in Jesus, Who shed His blood to seal the covenant with us. Thus giving us God's promises of - forgiveness for our sins, His Spirit indwelling us and an eternal loving relationship with Him.

I know the word covenant isn't used much in our society anymore, but the theme of covenant in the Bible is very meaningful. It gives us a beautiful view of how much God loves us and wants to be in a committed relationship with us. Covenant in the Bible may be thought of as the committed relationship from which God's love *(hesed)* becomes alive to us, like a marriage relationship. (Genesis 17:7; Psalm 106:43-45; Isaiah 54:10, 59:21; Matthew 26:26-29; 2 Corinthians 3:6).

Loving others is a must. God tells us and shows us how to love through His Word, with His Spirit (Romans 5:5; 1 Corinthians 13:4-7). We will never be able to *agape* love anyone fully, because it is a supernatural phenomenon coming from the God of love. But God does want to empower us to come as close to His love as humanly possible. Jesus tells us in John chapter thirteen that people will know we are His by our love for one another. So loving others makes us a witness for Jesus. Neat motivation to love, isn't it? *Read Ephesians 5:1-2; 1 John 4:19-21.*

> *A new commandment I give to you, that you love one another, even as I have loved you, that you also love one another. By this all men will know that you are My disciples, if you have love for one another. John 13:34-35 (NASB)*

Is there someone in your life you find hard to love? If so, ask Jesus to help you love that person.

What are your personal thoughts about how God loves you?

Exhortation: Rejoice over God's love for you.
It will never disappoint. It will always hold you tight.
It will give you a happily ever after eternity with love.

God is All-Loving and His Actions Prove It
~Day Twenty-Six~

God's love is defined by His actions

In many instances in our society, love has become just a hollow word, because we fail to put our love into action. God's love, in contrast, is filled with loving action.

> *...for I knew that You are a gracious and compassionate God, slow to anger and abundant in lovingkindness (hesed)...*
> *Jonah 4:2b (NASB)*

Let me ask you a few questions so you will clearly understand what I am meaning about actions of love. Do you have a spouse who gives you romantic gifts, but is never there for you? Have you had someone say she is doing something out of love for you, but what she is doing says she doesn't even like you? When words are said and gifts are given to show love, but they have no loving actions to back them up, we don't really feel or think we are loved, do we? Remember that old but true saying, "actions speak louder than words."

Some of God's loving actions

The Crucifixion. Before the Roman soldiers drove nails through Jesus' hands and feet to hang Him on a cross to execute Him like a common criminal - they stripped Him, mocked His claim to deity including placing a crown of thorns and a purple robe on Him, and they whipped and struck Him brutally. Jesus was also betrayed and denied by close friends, and then spit on, beaten, and condemned by the chief religious leaders. (Matthew 26:1-4, 47-75, 27:11-54).

> *But He was pierced through for our transgressions, He was crushed for our iniquities; the chastening for our well-being fell upon Him, and by His scourging we are healed. / But God demonstrates His own love toward us, in that while we were yet sinners, Christ died for us. Isaiah 53:5; Romans 5:8 (NASB)*

As Jesus hung on the cross, the world went dark for three hours, as He was forsaken by God the Father when He became our sin-offering. What happened during the darkness? God the Son felt a separation from God the Father that He had never known, as the God of perfect holiness allowed the Son of His triune Being to take the punishment for our sins upon Himself.

> *...darkness fell upon all the land...Jesus cried out with a loud voice, saying,... "MY GOD, MY GOD, WHY HAVE YOU FORSAKEN ME?" Matthew 27:45-46 (NASB)*

What comes to my mind now is the song: *Oh how He loves you and me... He gave His life what more could He give...* What comes to your mind?

The Resurrection. Yes, Jesus Christ died on the cross, but He did not remain dead. He rose from the dead three days later. (Matthew 27:57-61, 28:1-10). If Jesus had not risen from the dead, His death would have been just like the many thousands of other people who were crucified on a cross. Without Jesus' resurrection there would have been no victory over sin and death. Jesus' resurrection proved that He is God, and that He has the power to pay for our sins and to give us the certainty of our resurrection. (John 10:17-18; Romans 1:4; 1 Corinthians 15:3-8, 50-57).

In Texas, twenty-six innocent people were murdered as they worshipped our God. Because of God's death and resurrection, evil had no victory that day. As those beloved people died, they went immediately to Jesus. (John 11:25-26; 2 Corinthians 5:6-9). When the distress of life hits, which is often, the hope of the resurrection gives me peace and strength. How about you?

God's Word. God wanted the people He loved to know about Him and life, and the real history of the world from beginning to the end, so God through His Spirit inspired many different authors to write His Book (2 Peter 1:20-21). The golden thread of God's love throughout the Bible is Jesus Christ, and what He did for us (Psalm 119:41).

After Jesus' resurrection, He walked the earth for 40 days, then ascended back to heaven (Acts 1:3). One of the many things He did during this time was to walk with two of His disciples as He explained to them the things pertaining to Him throughout the Bible (Luke 24:13-32). You can tell by the story it was a life-changing experience for them.

<u>God's Creation.</u> God spoke, and creation unfolded day by day into the beautiful world He wanted for us. His creation is His work of love for us. (Psalm 33:5, 108:4, 119:64. 136: 1-9). God in fact created you to love you (John 3:16). Creation is a wonderful love story, isn't it?

> *You have granted me life and lovingkindness (hesed); And Your care has preserved my spirit. Job 10:12 (NASB)*

<u>God's love is personal towards you and me.</u> We can't say we love someone, until we have someone to love. You are God's someone to love. God's love is towards each one of us, as if we were God's only love. God loves you no matter what you have done or who you are. As you know, people's love has conditions. You do something wrong, and their love may stop. Yet God's love is different. He loved me before I was born, and has never stopped loving me even when I didn't know or care about Him. God's actions of love changed my life. What about your life?

> *...the Son of God, who loved me and gave Himself up for me. / The LORD appeared to him from afar, saying, I have loved you with an everlasting love; therefore I have drawn you with lovingkindness. Galatians 2:20b; Jeremiah 31:3 (NASB)*

~Life Application~

Love put in plain words

First Corinthians chapter thirteen has been called the Love
Chapter of the Bible. Below is the passage specifically
describing God's love.

> *Love is patient, love is kind and is not jealous; love does not
> brag and is not arrogant, does not act unbecomingly; it
> does not seek its own, is not provoked, does not take into
> account a wrong suffered, does not rejoice in
> unrighteousness, but rejoices with the truth; bears all
> things, believes all things, hopes all things, endures all
> things. 1 Corinthians 13:4-7 (NASB)*

Keep in mind God never asks you to do what He hasn't
done. So when you are asked to love others with these
loving qualities, Jesus has loved you that way. Just replace
the word love with Jesus: *Jesus is patient, Jesus is kind, and so
on.* Summarize 1 Corinthians 13:4-7 in your own words.

Now ask God to give you the ability and desire to love this
way.

Remember we are commanded to love God too! *Read Mark 12:29-31.* What are some ways you can show your love to God?

One of the ways I show my love to God is by memorizing His words, especially the Psalms. Memorizing allows Who God is and what He has done for me to become a part of my thoughts and my heart. My daughter-in-law told me to tell you here, to memorize Psalm 1. It is a Psalm that explains the importance of memorizing God's Word. Wise idea.

Exhortation: Trust God's loving embrace
to take care of you, and to deal with the thing
that is troubling you at just the right time.

The LORD says, "Can a woman forget her nursing child, And have no compassion on the son of her womb? Even these may forget, but I will not forget you. Behold, I have inscribed you on the palms of My hands..." Isaiah 49:8a, 15-16a

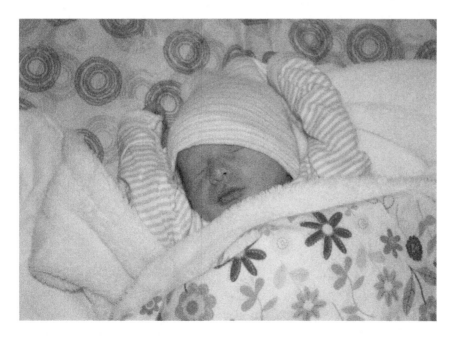

Week Seven

Days Twenty-Seven through Thirty

Day 27. The One True God is Our Loving Eternal Father
Day 28. The One True God is Our Loving Husband
Day 29. The One True God is Jesus Our Savior
Day 30. The One True God, Jesus, is Our Suffering Servant

~Notes~

The One True God - His Characteristics and Names

148

The One True God is Our Loving Eternal Father
~Day Twenty-Seven~

Our perfect Father

In Isaiah 9:6, God is called "*Eternal Father*." What do you think about when someone says, "father?" Do you have fond memories or memories of loneliness or possibly fear? No matter what your father was or is to you, your heavenly Father is the Father Who has and will always love and care for you (Matthew 6:26).

For clarity, we are going to look at God being our Father from the framework of the Trinity. (Remember, on day four in this daily devotional we discussed the Trinity.) The One True God chose to reveal to us *His triune nature* in three persons: God the Father, God the Son, and God the Holy Spirit. Each person has their role in the Trinity. The Father's role of directing, sending, and originating is similar to fatherhood. The Son's role is obeying, going as the Father sends, and revealing the One True God to us. The Holy Spirit's role is our Helper. An example of their roles in our salvation: God the Father planned it, sent the Son to accomplish it, and then had the Holy Spirit give us new spiritual life and the power to live that new life.[1] (John 14:8-11, 26; Galatians 1:3-4; Titus 3:4-7).

Our Father - our dad

God our Father will always be there for you. When my mother died of cancer when I was five, I went to live with my father's mother, my grandmother. My father lived with us, but stayed away a lot. I felt lonely, even deserted, at times. In Psalm 27:10, King David stated his parents had forsaken him, but God had not. Keep in mind, your heavenly Father is always there for you even if your parents might not have been. He is the type of father you can easily call dad, because He will never give up on you, even if you do awful things.

> For my father and my mother have forsaken me, but the LORD
> will take me up. Psalm 27:10 (NASB)

Aren't you glad your God will never desert you or give up on you?

The love of the Father

I believe a mother's sacrificial love for her child is the closest human love to God's love. Yet, God tells us in Isaiah 49:15, His compassion is even stronger than a mothers. In Sudan, a mother had a son, who had a cleft lip. The village people, even the woman's family turned against her, because they thought anyone who had a deformed child was cursed. However, the woman loved her son and lovingly cared for him, even when everyone else wanted her to abandon him. She finally found him help through Samaritan's Purse. Our heavenly Father's love and a mother's love give life, a safe refuge, strength, joy and hope for the future.

Can a woman forget her nursing child, and have no compassion on the son of her womb? Even these may forget, but I will not forget you. Behold, I have inscribed you on the palms of My hands; your walls are continually before Me. Isaiah 49:15-16 (NASB)

Does Isaiah 49:15-16 make you feel wanted and cherished by our God? Does His compassion towards you give you joy, strength and hope?

Jesus puts us in His family

The moment you believe in Jesus is the moment you become a child of God. Have you ever truly thought about what that means?

But as many as received Him, to them He gave the right to become children of God, even to those who believe in His name, who were born not of blood, nor of the will of the flesh, nor of the will of man, but of God. John 1:12-13 (NASB)

Romans chapter eight talks about how God sent the Holy Spirit to live within us, which enables us to be His adopted children. The Spirit gives us an eternal family relationship with God and an awareness of that relationship. Before the Spirit is dwelling in us, God loves us, but He is separated from us and is not in a relationship with us.

For you have not received a spirit of slavery leading to fear again, but you have received a spirit of adoption as sons by which we cry out, "Abba! Father!" The Spirit Himself testifies with our spirit that we are children of God, and if children, heirs also, heirs of God and fellow heirs with Christ... Romans 8:15-17 (NASB)

As God's adopted children: All debts from sin have been cancelled, we gain the full rights and privileges of a daughter or son of God on this earth, and we inherit all the benefits, riches, and promises of heaven (Ephesians 1:3-14). Amazing family that we live in as Christians, isn't it?

~Life Application~

You are God's child

When you think of adopting a child, you think of a parent choosing to love and make a child her own. Consider this marvelous truth: God, the Creator and Self-Existent One, Who is Sovereign over the entire universe - chose you to be His beloved daughter or son (Ephesians 1:3-5). This truth has always encouraged me to live in my eternal Father's embrace.

How do you feel about God choosing you to be His child?

Does it make you feel special, even adored?

<u>Your Father's comfort.</u> Many fathers either don't know how to comfort or just don't want to. Our heavenly Father is a father that comforts His children abundantly in every affliction. *Read 2 Corinthians 1:2-5.*

Explain God's comfort for you from 2 Corinthians 1:2-5.

<u>Communication with your Father.</u> When you need a father to give you advice, shouldn't you seek God? Remember Who He is, and that He has wanted to be your loving Father from times past. Prayer is very important to God your Father; He loves for you to talk with Him, and wants to answer your prayers with good gifts. *Read Psalm 4:1, 5:1-3, Matthew 7:7-11; Luke 11:9-13.*

Do you pray to God your Father? If you don't pray, ask God to get you chatting with Him. Believe me, He will answer. If you do pray, describe when, where and how you tend to pray.

I have found if I want to be communicating with God, I need to start my day with the thought and reality that God is with me. Then my prayer life that day seems to follow my mindset and I just naturally talk with Him throughout the day. So I try to have a prayer time in the morning. I have also made meal time prayer more than a thank God for my food, but a time to specifically call to Him. I figure I desire and need to eat, so I should have the same attitude about prayer. (Colossians 4:2). 5 –

Exhortation: Relax and enjoy being your heavenly Father's child. He will always love you, be there for you and never give up on you.

The One True God is
Our Loving Husband
~Day Twenty-Eight~

Our loving Husband

As Christians, we are the bride of Jesus Christ. Some of you have a husband who doesn't love you, so having a loving husband is hard to imagine. Some of you are simply not married, or are a husband yourself, so you are probably a little lost here. The rest of us, who are married, might have loving husbands, but as life is, no one can love us perfectly. No matter who we are, Jesus is our loving Husband, Who loves us like no human can. He is so glad we are His bride, He literally rejoices over us (Zephaniah 3:17; Hebrews 12:2). Devoted God, isn't He?

> *...And as the bridegroom rejoices over the bride, so your God will rejoice over you. / Let us rejoice and be glad and give the glory to Him, for the marriage of the Lamb (Jesus) has come and His bride has made herself ready. Isaiah 62:5; Revelation 19:7 (NASB)*

Two types of relationships

Our relationship with God at times is portrayed in His Word by using the husband-wife relationship and the parent-child relationship. Both the husband-wife and the parent-child relationships depict God's heartfelt longing to be in a close relationship with us. Yesterday, we discussed the parent-child relationship; today it will be the husband-wife relationship.

The prophet Hosea in the Old Testament writes about both of these family relationships, to allow us to understand God's heart desire for intimacy with us. In Ephesians chapter five, the husband-wife relationship is used to paint a picture of us as Jesus Christ's wife as a corporate Body (His Church), as well as each of us individually (Ephesians 5:25-32).

> *And I will betroth you to Me forever... in lovingkindness and in compassion, and I will betroth you to Me in faithfulness. Then you will know the Lord. Hosea 2:19-20 (NASB)*

Answers about God as our husband

How long has God your husband loved you? In Ephesians chapter one, God chose you to be His even before the world and universe were created. God has been waiting to show you His love from eternity past. We could say, God's love for you started in eternity, so you have never been unloved by God. (Isaiah 30:18a; Jeremiah 31:3; Galatians 2:20b).

> *Remember, O LORD, Your compassion and Your lovingkindnesses, for they have been from of old (everlasting). / ...who has blessed us with every spiritual blessing in the heavenly places in Christ, just as He chose us in Him before the foundation of the world...in love... Psalm 25:6; Ephesians 1:3-4 (NASB)*

Did you know Jesus Christ, your husband, had to sacrifice
His very life to marry you? Remember the state we were in
before we became Christians? We were separated from
Jesus because of sin (Isaiah 59:2). So Jesus, our would-be
husband, couldn't even have a relationship with us, much
less marry us. He could only love us from afar. However,
our Bridegroom's sacrificial death set us free from our sins
so we can be eternally His. (Romans 5:10-11; Revelation 1:5).
Beautiful love story, isn't it?

> *...Christ also loved you, and gave Himself up for us, an*
> *offering and a sacrifice to God. Ephesians 5:2 (NASB)*

How valuable are you to Jesus your husband? You can tell
what value someone is to a person, by how much he is
willing to give or sacrifice for the person. I know some of
you feel like you aren't worth much at all, because of the lies
you were told as a child or as an adult, or both. What you
need to remember is, your value to the One True God is
beyond cost. It is priceless. He gave His very life to make
you His bride (Galatians 2:20b).

> *...knowing that you were not redeemed with perishable*
> *things like silver or gold from your futile way of life*
> *inherited from your forefathers, but with precious blood, as*
> *of a lamb unblemished and spotless, the blood of Christ.*
> *1 Peter 1:18-19 (NASB)*

Do you feel discouraged, hopeless or depressed sometimes?
Maybe you feel insignificant even invisible in some
situations? I know I can. Women especially can feel
unattractive, perhaps even ugly, because of the world's

expectations on their outward appearance. Frankly as I get old, if I zero in on my wrinkles, etc., I certainly don't feel very beautiful. I am sure many of you can relate because life is life. Yet, there is a life-changing answer to our heartfelt psychological and physical struggles, Jesus Christ. Remember dear ones, you have been set free by Jesus to live in His joy, grace and confidence, as His glorious bride. Knowing I am very much loved and esteemed by Jesus has given me the desire and resolve to live as He sees me, as His beloved just right bride. (Isaiah 61:1-3, 7, 10; Ephesians 5:25-27; Jude 24-25). How about you?

> *For the LORD takes pleasure in His people; He will beautify the afflicted ones with salvation. Psalm 149:4 (NASB)*

God is our faithful husband

I am blessed to have a faithful and loving husband. But some of you do not. So it is just natural to feel God will be disloyal. I promise you, God will be faithful and loyal to you. His love and faithfulness aren't bound by what we do, they are bound by Who He is. Remember, God's love is a loyal, faithful love. God has no intention of not staying committed to you. He gave His life to be with you.

If we are honest with ourselves, we are not the perfect wife. We go against God quite often by doing exactly what we want and not what God wants. Yet, God is our loving and devoted husband, Who is always patient, forgiving and compassionate towards us (Isaiah 54:4-10). I think He is the perfect husband. Do you?

I will rejoice greatly in the LORD, My soul will exult in my God; For He has clothed me with garments of salvation, He has wrapped me with a robe of righteousness, As a bridegroom decks himself with a garland, And as a bride adorns herself with her jewels. Isaiah 61:10 (NASB)

~Life Application~

Imagine meeting Jesus, your Bridegroom, in heaven

As we all know too well, we can't escape death. Yet, as Christians, death takes us into the loving presence of the One True God.

This is what I imagine my first day in heaven will be like from what I know from scripture: When I leave this world and open my eyes in the next, I will see Jesus standing there with a glory that is beyond earthly description. His face will shine like the sun, but even with its brilliance, I will see a smile on His face because I am His joy. I believe I will fall on my knees in awe, and He will put His right hand on me and say, "Do not be afraid; I am the One Who has loved you and have been waiting for you." He will take me to see my dwelling in eternity that He has been preparing and my heavenly inheritance that I inherited because of Him. As I am with Him I will feel His kindness and grace embracing me; and realize I am wearing wedding clothes that are as beautiful as the heavenly glory all around me. I will feel a peace and happiness that I could never have had on our earth. I will look up into my Bridegroom's eyes, and for the first time fully understand His love for me.

Someday you and I will literally meet the One True God face to face. *Read John 14:1-3, 27; 1 Corinthians 13:10-12, 15:42-49; 2 Corinthians 5:1-8; Ephesians 1:3-4, 2:7; Hebrews 12:1-2; Jude 24 -25; Revelation 1:12-19, 19:7-8.* Write some insights from these passages about being in heaven with Jesus.

From the above passages, which passage gives you the most hope and joy about heaven?

Exhortation: Jesus your Husband is always near, so there's nothing to fear. Walk with Him. His strong and loving embrace will eternally surround you and be your sanctuary.

The One True God is Jesus Our Savior
~Day Twenty-Nine~

Our Savior

We needed a savior, so the One True God became our Savior (1 Timothy 4:10). Jesus Christ didn't die just in case we needed a savior. The awful truth is everyone needed to be saved from their sins; if there was no savior we would all be paying for our own sins in hell. The word savior means: a deliverer, preserver, one who saves from danger or destruction, and brings into a state of prosperity and happiness.[1]

The One True God willingly put on flesh and blood, and as a result became our Savior to deliver us from the all-consuming power, judgment, punishment and guilt of sin, and to give us His righteousness. God also brings prosperity and happiness through a never-ending relationship with Him, and the many promises inherited from Him. (Philippians 3:20-21). Is Jesus your Savior?

> *...Is it not I, the* LORD*? And there is no other God besides Me, a righteous God and a Savior; there is none except Me. Turn to Me and be saved, all the ends of the earth... / But when the kindness of God our Savior and His love for mankind appeared, He saved us, not on the basis of deeds which we have done in righteousness, but according to His mercy, by ... renewing by the Holy Spirit, whom He poured out upon us richly through Jesus Christ our Savior, so that being justified by His grace we would be made heirs according to the hope of eternal life. Isaiah 45:21-22; Titus 3:4-7 (NASB)*

The name Jesus

The name Jesus means Savior. The angel told Joseph, Mary's husband, in a dream, to name the Child that was conceived by the Holy Spirit, "Jesus." This is because He will save His people from their sins.

> ...an angel of the Lord appeared to him in a dream, saying, "Joseph...do not be afraid to take Mary as your wife; for the Child who has been conceived in her is of the Holy Spirit. She will bear a Son; and you shall call His name Jesus, for He will save His people from their sins." Now all this took place to fulfill what was spoken by the Lord through the prophet: "BEHOLD, THE VIRGIN SHALL BE WITH CHILD AND SHALL BEAR A SON, AND THEY SHALL CALL HIS NAME IMMANUEL," which translated means, "GOD WITH US." And Joseph...did as the angel of the Lord commanded him, and took Mary as his wife, but kept her a virgin until she gave birth to a Son; and he called His name Jesus.
> Matthew 1:18-25 (NASB)

When Jesus' name is mentioned, many times there is a strong reaction. Most people recognize Jesus and countless others love Him, but some are put off by Him, or despise Him, and some refuse to believe He is Who He said He is - God. Yes, there is something about Jesus' name that brings a reaction like no other name does.

In Philippians chapter two we are told that Jesus' name is highly exalted above every name. God made the name "Jesus" to awaken our very heart and soul (Philippians 2:9-11). I think you understand, this is because of Who Jesus is, and not just the name itself. What reaction do you have to Jesus' name?

Jesus the conqueror of sin

Jesus our Savior saves us from all sins. We don't sin in a vacuum. Every sin, either ours or someone else's, can affect us, others, and even our environment. Quite a bit of our suffering is caused by others sinning. So when you feel like no one cares if that person or that group is being malicious towards you, remember, Jesus sees it and cared so much, He died to deliver you from the world's evil. (Galatians 1:3-4).

As our Savior, God didn't just save us from our sins, but He brings contentment and a victorious life to us. When your well-being is being threatened, or possibly your very life, God is there to save you (Psalm 3:3-8). If you are struggling with a job, or perhaps your finances, God will sustain you (Philippians 4:11-13). Maybe you are feeling miserable, overwhelmed or anxious from emotional or physical struggles, then go to God. He wants to support you (Philippians 4:5b-7).

> *...Christ Jesus is He who died, yes, rather who was raised, who is at the right hand of God, who also intercedes for us. Who will separate us from the love of Christ? Will tribulation, or distress, or persecution, or famine, or nakedness, or peril, or sword? ...But in all these things we overwhelmingly conquer through Him who loved us. Romans 8:34-37 (NASB)*

Because of my Savior, Jesus, I have conquered my lack of self-confidence, and many more weaknesses and sins in my life. I can sincerely say He has helped me triumph over many of the things that held me back from being what I should be in Him. What has Jesus helped you conquer?

The LORD of hosts

God is called "the LORD of hosts" or "LORD Almighty" in the Old Testament. This name has the idea of a deliverer with might and power in it. God is our powerful King and warrior, Who rules the entire universe, yet He is ready to deliver us at the cost of His own life. (Zechariah 4:6).[2]

> *It will become a sign and a witness to the LORD of hosts in the land of Egypt; for they will cry to the LORD because of oppressors, and He will send them a Savior and a Champion, and He will deliver them. Isaiah 19:20 (NASB)*

What does it mean to you that the One True God, is the LORD of Hosts, your mighty deliverer?

Immanuel

Immanuel is a name of Jesus. Do you remember what the name Immanuel means? Jesus is called Immanuel, because He is the One True God, Who became flesh to literally be with us (Isaiah 7:14; Matthew 1:23). God taking on flesh to be with me certainly makes me feel wanted. You too?

~Life Application~

Our Savior who delivers us

God your deliverer is described in Psalm ninety-one. *Read Psalm 91.* From this passage, describe how God delivers and protects us.

When my son was in Iraq, I was constantly praying for him. God used Psalm ninety-one to reassure me He would deliver and defend my son from harm, and God did.

What does it mean to you that the One True God is your Savior? Take some time to thank Jesus for being your Savior.

Exhortation: Our Savior saved us to live abundantly -
doing all there is to do through Him.
Don't live for the world.

The One True God, Jesus, is Our Suffering Servant
~Day Thirty~

Jesus our Servant

A name of God that has always amazed me is Servant. To be our suffering Servant, Jesus Christ willingly went from the supremacy of His glorified state to the humiliating state of a man. Becoming a man, Jesus set aside His rights, self-interests, glory and splendor as the One True God, but He did not set aside His deity.[1] I feel a lot of people don't really comprehend or even recognize the incredible humiliation that Jesus undertook to deal with us and our sins. If they did, why wouldn't the whole world be loving and serving the God Who loves and serves them?

Do you wonder what Jesus looks like in His glorified state? Isaiah, a prophet in the Old Testament must have had a very close relationship with the One True God. This is because Isaiah saw amazing glimpses of Jesus Christ in both His glorified state and as our suffering Servant. He wrote about these glimpses in the book of Isaiah. (Isaiah 7:14, 9:6-7, 52:13 - 53:12).

> ...I (Isaiah) saw the Lord sitting on a throne, lofty and exalted, with the train of His robe filling the temple. Seraphim (angels) stood above Him... And one called out to another and said, "Holy, Holy, Holy, is the LORD of hosts, the whole earth is full of His glory..." Then I said, "Woe is me... For my eyes have seen the King, the LORD of hosts." / These things Isaiah said because he saw His glory, and he spoke of Him (Jesus). Isaiah 6:1-5; John 12:41 (NASB)

What Jesus gave up

What Jesus gave up to be our Servant is best described in Philippians 2:6-8.[1]

> *...who, although He (Jesus) existed in the form of God, did not regard equality with God a thing to be grasped, but emptied Himself, taking the form of a bond-servant, and being made in the likeness of men. And being found in appearance as a man, He humbled Himself by becoming obedient to the point of death, even death on a cross. Philippians 2:6-8 (NASB)*

The meaning of Philippians 2:6-8:

In Philippians 2:6 the phrase *although He existed in the form of God* - the Greek word *form* refers to the outward expression which a person gives of his inmost nature. In other words, *form* means nature and character, not shape, as we would think. This means Jesus is in the *form* of the One True God (John 14:7–11).[1]

In Philippians 2:7 the phrase *but emptied Himself* - the Greek word *emptied* means to empty oneself, to divest oneself of rightful dignity by descending to an inferior condition, to abase or humiliate oneself.[1]

In Philippians 2:7-8a the phrase *taking the form of a bond-servant and being made in the likeness of men. And being found in appearance as a man* - means when Jesus took on the new inmost nature of a man at His incarnation, His outward expression as a man was that of a servant.[1]

Just consider Who Jesus is, and then realize that He literally divested Himself of His glory, power and privilege as God, and voluntarily allowed Himself to be humiliated as our suffering servant to the point of even dying on a cross. This is an incredible truth that still amazes me. I don't know about you, but I try my best not to be humiliated. So the fact that the One True God was willing to be humiliated for me, humbles me. It makes me want to love and serve Him as He does me.

It's important to understand: Jesus becoming man didn't eliminate His deity. He had two natures after His incarnation, that of absolute deity and absolute humanity. After His resurrection, He laid aside His form as a suffering servant, but He still remains fully God and fully man for the rest of eternity.[1]

What are your thoughts on Philippians 2:6-8?

Jesus came to serve and not to be served

In Matthew 20:17-28, Jesus was explaining to His 12 disciples how God measured greatness. They thought of greatness just like we think of greatness today, which is having wealth, prestige, and power over people. But Jesus contradicted their views on greatness, and stated greatness comes from being a servant, thinking of others first. As Christians, we need to follow Jesus' example, and be great by serving too. (Matthew 20:25-28).

...just as the Son of Man (another name for Jesus) did not come to be served, but to serve, and to give His life a ransom for many. Matthew 20:28 (NASB)

The comings of Jesus Christ

Jesus Christ first came to this earth as a suffering servant, as we just learned. At His second coming to earth, He will be coming in all His glory and splendor, as King of kings and Lord of lords, to be our eternal sovereign ruler. One of Jesus' names is the Son of Man; this name emphasizes both His first coming to this earth that has already happened, and His second coming which is still in the future. (Daniel 7:13-14; Revelation 22:20-21).

~Life Application~

Being a servant

The One True God performs the most selfless of tasks in John chapter thirteen. Jesus' menial service of washing feet surprised His 12 disciples, because by then they knew Him as the Lord. When we reflect on Who Jesus is, and that the hosts in heaven instantaneously fall down and worship Him, I understand His disciples' surprise. Who would imagine the Creator, the Sovereign King of the universe, would stoop to serve us? *Read John 8:6-11, 13:1-17; Revelation 1:5-19, 5:8-14, 19:6-16.*

What does it mean to you that the One True God is your suffering Servant?

To serve or not to serve? In John chapter thirteen Jesus states, you are blessed if you serve people, even the ones that are not pleasant to serve. Washing people's very dirty and smelly feet surely wasn't pleasant. Jesus washing His disciple's feet reminds me that I need to follow His example and serve.

Prayerfully think of ways and write them down, on how you can serve your family, friends, and others better.

I have a friend who has made some bad decisions which have greatly affected her life. It would be so much easier for me to just give up on our friendship, and I have thought of doing that, but if I did I would not be a servant or friend.

Exhortation: Serve your God,
Who loved you so much
He stepped out of eternity to serve you.

Week Eight

Days Thirty-One through Thirty-Three

~Notes~

Jesus the Lamb of God
~Day Thirty-One~

Our Lamb is our God

The only sacrifice that can secure our salvation is the sacrifice of the Lamb of God. This is because He is the One True God.

> ...(John the Baptist said of Jesus), "Behold, the Lamb of God who takes away the sin of the world!" John 1:29 (NASB)

The Old Testament revealed the need for a sacrifice (a lamb) to cover our sins. In Exodus chapter twelve we are told flawless lambs were to be chosen and sacrificed during the Feast of the Passover. The blood of the lambs would be used to cover the peoples' sin, delivering them from death at that time. Another example is in Isaiah chapter fifty-three, where hundreds of years before Jesus' life and death, He is described as our Lamb.

The Lamb of God is our substitute

I think by now you understand how destructive sin is! It took death to pay for even one sin. Therefore because of God's love for us, He chose sacrificial blood as payment for a person's life. This allowed us to have a substitute die for our sins. (Leviticus 17:11).

In the Old Testament, God revealed to the Jews it was necessary for them to consistently shed the blood of innocent animals (their substitute) to cover their sins. The sacrifice of the animal would become their substitute when the guilty person laid his hand on its head, signifying the innocent animal was dying for him. The animal sacrifices only brought temporary forgiveness. (Leviticus 1:4, 4:32-35).

The bloody Old Testament animal sacrifices made people realize how awful sin was, and that it was impossible to cleanse their sin and change their evil hearts by those sacrifices. It became apparent to them that only God could. (Hebrews10:1-4).

Jesus' blood is the only blood that removes, not just covers, our sins. God didn't take pleasure in animal sacrifices. He knew only His one sacrifice - His death - His blood had the power to be the substitute that would permanently cleanse our sin and change our hearts. (Hebrews 10:4-18).

Jesus owed us nothing, yet because of His love for us, He paid off what we owed Him from our sins by becoming our Lamb. He died in our place. We now put our hand of faith on Jesus, our substitute, to gain forever forgiveness. Incredible forgiveness we live in, isn't it?

> *To Him (Jesus) who loves us and released us from our sins by His blood. / ...that through His name (Jesus) everyone who believes in Him receives forgiveness of sins. / ...knowing that you were not redeemed with perishable things like silver or gold...but with precious blood, as of a lamb unblemished and spotless, the blood of Christ. Revelation 1:5b; Acts 10:43; 1 Peter 1:18-19 (NASB)*

Jesus chose to be our Lamb

In Russia at the height of the cold war, a colonel had just moments to choose whether the signal going off at the Soviet military early warning facility was a false alarm or a real US nuclear attack. Because of God's loving sovereignty, the colonel made the right decision (it was a false alarm) and saved millions of lives around the world from his choice.

Jesus Christ at any moment could have chosen to stop His suffering and crucifixion, yet He chose not to. Jesus was our sacrificial Lamb because He chose to yield up His body to death. His sacrifice was most definitely the right decision to save everyone who chooses to be saved. (Revelation 5:8-14). Jesus' sacrifice took place at a point in time, but stands over all history to cover all sins.

Have you chosen Jesus? It's a choice you need to make. If you don't make that choice, you will end up eternally away from God. And believe me that is not what you want.

Jesus the Passover Lamb

About 2000 years ago in Jerusalem, the Passover was being celebrated. People were there to sacrifice their Passover lambs to cover their own sins. Outside Jerusalem, on a hill that looked and smelled like death, the Roman soldiers were crucifying three men. Two of the men were criminals and deserved death. But the third was God Himself, being nailed to the cross because of our sins. Jesus Christ is our perfect Passover Lamb, our substitute (1 Corinthians 5:7b).

Our Lamb, chose to take the punishment we deserved upon Himself, and as a result His blood covered all of our sins, so we can now have a pure heart, a clear conscience and a new life with our God. In other words, all things in your life are new in Jesus. (2 Corinthians 5:17, 21; Hebrews 10:19-22).

> *...namely, that God was in Christ reconciling the world to Himself, not counting their trespasses against them...*
> *2 Corinthians 5:19 (NASB)*

Frankly, it is just hard to entirely explain and even grasp the magnitude of what Jesus did for us, isn't it? As the refrain of a song exclaims, *"Amazing love! How can it be that Thou, my God, shouldst die for me."*

The favorite name

We tend to call ourselves our favorite name, whether it is our formal name or a nickname, don't we? While teaching the Book of Revelation, I realized something very special. Out of all the names Jesus could be known by in Revelation, such as Creator, LORD, I AM or King of kings, His favorite name is The Lamb. It is used 30 times in the book. Why is this? It is because Jesus, as our Lamb, made it possible for us to be with Him. The fact that Jesus in eternity uses The Lamb as His favorite name, makes me realize how much He truly rejoices over being with you and me. (Zephaniah 3:17; Hebrews 12:2). This is certainly a wonderful reality to ponder.

~Life Application~

Jesus, the Son of Man - explained

The Son of Man is another title Jesus was fond of for Himself, and is the name He called Himself the most when He was on this earth. (It is used over 80 times in the Gospels.) So what does this name of God mean? Son of Man comes from a prophecy given to Daniel where the future eternal sovereign rule of Jesus Christ on this earth is foretold (Daniel 7:13-14). This name emphasizes both Jesus' humanity and His humiliation as our suffering Servant and Lamb (Matthew 17:22-23, 20:28), as well as His deity and eternal glorified state. (Matthew 25:31, 26:64).[1]

Jesus explained in the Gospels that as the Son of Man, He came to serve, suffer, and to give His life as a ransom for us, bringing the guarantee of eternal life and resurrection for all who want it. Jesus further explained that in the future, the Son of Man will come again in all His glorious majesty, power and sovereignty to rule this earth in peace and love, and in righteousness and justice too. (Isaiah 9:6-7).

Why do you think Jesus used the name the Son of Man more than any other name when He was on this earth?

What does it mean to you that someday, maybe soon, the One True God will come again to this earth in bodily form, not as a servant, but as the King of kings?

What does it mean to you personally that Jesus is your Lamb?

An illustration that keeps coming to my mind is: A father and daughter were out in the woods collecting berries. The father out of the corner of his eye saw a dog coming towards them that was acting very odd. He knew immediately the dog had rabies. (At the time there was no vaccine for rabies, so it was certain death if you were bitten by an animal with rabies.) Since there was no tree near them, with no hesitation even though he knew the horrible death that awaited him, he lifted his beloved child on to his shoulders so that there would be no chance she would be bitten. The dog bit the man until he could save his daughter by putting her in a tree. The father willing sacrificed his life for his child. Jesus willingly sacrificed His life for me by becoming my Lamb. He saved me from the certain horrors of eternal death and punishment, to give me life in heaven.

Exhortation: Jesus, your Lamb sacrificed His all for you to give life to you. Every step you take, every word you speak, every breath you breathe should be for Him and in Him.

The One True God Lives within Us
~Day Thirty-Two~

The Holy Spirit and us

As Christians an amazing thing happens - the One True God comes to dwell within us. Before we were Christians, the Holy Spirit did not live in us, so we were in spiritual darkness or spiritually dead (John 3:19; Ephesians 2:1). Yet, His Spirit was still always there protecting, leading, and wooing us to God (Psalm 139:7-10). When you believe in Jesus Christ, the Holy Spirit comes to live within you - giving you spiritual life, and a glorious relationship with the triune God (John 3:6-8; Romans 8:9-11; Titus 3:4-7).

> *Jesus said... "I will ask the Father, and He will give you another Helper, that He may be with you forever; that is the Spirit of truth, whom the world cannot receive, because it does not see Him or know Him, but you know Him because He abides with you and will be in you." John 14:16-17 (NASB)*

In the Old Testament times, the Holy Spirit didn't live in all God's followers, but only a select few. The Holy Spirit living in all God's people was a promise that was fulfilled after Jesus' death and resurrection. (Acts 1:4-9, 2:1-18, 32-33).

Every time I think about the fact the One True God lives within me, it takes me back to realizing how much God wants to be with me. Yes, it's an amazing relationship we are in with our God, isn't it?

The Holy Spirit seals us

In Him (Jesus), you also, after listening to the message of truth, the gospel of your salvation - having also believed, you were <u>sealed</u> in Him with the Holy Spirit of promise... Ephesians 1:13 (NASB)

We are sealed in Jesus by the Holy Spirit at the moment we believe in Jesus. The word *sealed* in the Greek language means: to set a seal upon, mark with a seal. In scripture, a seal symbolizes a finished transaction, ownership, and security. When something is sealed, everything is in order. It is the final approval of that transaction. When the Spirit seals us, it signifies that the eternal transaction of payment for our sins has been completely and perfectly finished in Jesus (John 19:30). We are now His, and are eternally secure in Him, because we have His seal upon us.[1] What does it mean to you that you are sealed by the Spirit?

The Holy Spirit is our pledge

...who is given as a <u>pledge</u> of our inheritance, with a view to the redemption of God's own possession, to the praise of His glory. Ephesians 1:14 (NASB)

The Holy Spirit is our pledge from God. The word *pledge* even today in Greece can mean engagement ring. God's Spirit is His symbol of love given to us so we can know without a shadow of a doubt we are His forever, and that every promise given to us from God is guaranteed. Instead of wearing the love symbol on our finger, we wear Him in our hearts.[2] (2 Corinthians 1:21–22, 3:3). Isn't this a beautiful illustration from God, showing you He loves you?

The Holy Spirit reveals God's thoughts to us

Have you ever found yourself thinking something like, "I wish I could know their thoughts?" I sure have. As you know, it is impossible to know what a person is really thinking unless they tell you. Only God's Spirit knows God's thoughts. Yet, amazingly He reveals His thoughts to us through His Spirit. The Spirit indwelling us teaches us to know God, His Word and His will, and He gives us the wisdom to understand God's spiritual truths including our many spiritual blessings.

> *But just as it is written, "THINGS WHICH EYE HAS NOT SEEN AND EAR HAS NOT HEARD, AND which HAVE NOT ENTERED THE HEART OF MAN, ALL THAT GOD HAS PREPARED FOR THOSE WHO LOVE HIM." For to us God revealed them through the Spirit; for the Spirit searches all things, even the depths of God. For who among men knows the thoughts of a man except the spirit of the man which is in him? Even so the thoughts of God no one knows except the Spirit of God. Now we have received, not the spirit of the world, but the Spirit who is from God, so that we may know the things freely given to us by God, which things we also speak, not in words taught by human wisdom, but in those taught by the Spirit, combining spiritual thoughts with spiritual words. 1 Corinthians 2:9-13 (NASB)*

The Holy Spirit gives us God's power

Do you feel spiritually wimpy at times? I know I can. Yet, it is a feeling we really shouldn't have, because the power of the universe lives within us (Acts 1:8; Ephesians 3:16, 20). So for heaven's sake, ask the Spirit to empower you to live for God (Zechariah 4:6).

The Holy Spirit and God's love

God has poured His love within us and continues to flood our hearts with His love through His Spirit. We know of God's love because the Spirit lives within us. (Ephesians 3:16-20). Loving reality, isn't it?

> *...hope does not disappoint, because the love of God has been poured out within our hearts through the Holy Spirit who was given to us. Romans 5:5 (NASB)*

I think many of you are familiar with the dove as a symbol of the Holy Spirit (Luke 3:21-22). Our yard is full of doves. A dove couple made a nest in our front yard, and were lovingly watching over their eggs. My husband heard loud squawks one day, and went out to see the two doves flying at a bobcat to protect their eggs. We both realized the doves were willing to give their lives for their eggs. The Spirit of the One True God hovers over us and in us with His ever present love for us, and faithfully protects us.

What are your feelings about the Holy Spirit living in you?

~Life Application~

The Holy Spirit leading us

The Holy Spirit doesn't want us to stay as immature babies in Jesus Christ, controlled by our sinful desires or flesh. So the Spirit works to transform you into a mature Christian; one that acts very much like Jesus. (1 Corinthians 3:1-3; Ephesians 4:13-15). The Spirit will slowly but surely mature us, but we need to choose to cooperate with Him. We cooperate with the Spirit by allowing Him to lead us.

Here are some basic Christian principles we should be doing so the Spirit can lead us:

1. Faith/belief/trust in God gives us the Spirit and allows the Spirit to lead us. (Proverbs 3:5-6; Romans 15:13; Ephesians 1:13; Hebrews 11:6).

2. When we love God and others, the Spirit is leading. (Mark 12:29-31; Romans 5:5).

3. The Spirit leads us using His Word, so we need to be learning it. (Psalm 119:11, 105; 2 Timothy 3:16-17; 2 Peter 1:21).

4. Talk to God and listen to Him through His Word; His Spirit will lead you. (Psalm 143:10; Luke 11:9-13; John 14:26, 16:13-15; Romans 8:26-27).

5. Ask the Spirit to examine your life to get sin out of your life. Disobeying God means the Spirit isn't leading in that area. (Psalm 139:23-24; Proverbs 28:13).

God gave us a handy list in Galatians 5:22-23, so we can check our lives to see if we are being led by His Spirit, or by our own flesh (sinful desires). If you have the fruit of the Spirit in your life, that means you are allowing the Spirit to lead you. *Read Galatians 5:16-26.*

> *But the fruit of the Spirit is love, joy, peace, patience, kindness, goodness, faithfulness, gentleness, self-control ... If we live by the Spirit, let us also walk by the Spirit ... Galatians 5:22-25 (NASB)*

Being led by the Holy Spirit is like walking with the Spirit. Walking with the Spirit is similar to walking with someone - you are going in the same direction, there is a connection and sharing, and you are taking steps together to reach a common goal. The Holy Spirit's desire is to lead you, so when you won't let Him, well to be frank, you are then walking away from what God wants. (Romans 8:4).

I believe no one is led by the Spirit all the time, but to be like Jesus we need the Spirit to be leading us most of the time. Who is leading you most of the time, the Spirit or sin? Remember, He absolutely wants to lead your life. So ask for His help, He is our Helper. (Psalm 143:10).

What are your thoughts about the Holy Spirit leading you?

Exhortation: Trust in the Holy Spirit. He will give you wisdom and fill your innermost being with serenity. Listen to His quiet voice as He leads you through His Word.

The LORD is my shepherd, I shall not want. He makes me lie down in green pastures; He leads me beside quiet waters. He restores my soul; He guides me in the paths of righteousness... Psalm 23:1-3

The One True God - His Characteristics and Names

The One True God is
Our Good Shepherd
~Day Thirty-Three~

Our true Shepherd

God in His infinite love and wisdom knew we needed a shepherd. The One True God is this Shepherd. He came to guide and protect, and to give us exactly what we need in this troubling world. God dying for our sins allowed Him to lovingly care for us as a shepherd would.

> *Behold the Lord GOD will come with might, with His arm ruling for Him...Like a shepherd He will tend His flock, in His arm He will gather the lambs and carry them in His bosom; He will gently lead the nursing ewes. / All of us like sheep have gone astray, each of us has turned to his own way; but the LORD has caused the iniquity of us all, to fall on Him. / For you were continually straying like sheep, but now you have returned to the Shepherd and Guardian of your souls. / They will hunger no longer, nor thirst anymore; nor will the sun beat down on them, nor any heat; for the Lamb in the center of the throne will be their shepherd, and will guide them to springs of the water of life; and God will wipe every tear from their eyes. Isaiah 40:10-11, 53:6; 1 Peter 2:25; Revelation 7:16-17 (NASB)*

A shepherd was leading his sheep to fresh range grass when a wild dog tried to kill a lamb. The shepherd with his rod scared it off, then lifted up the lamb to comfort and heal it. I certainly act like a sheep - lost, afraid, and needing to be shown the way. We are all like sheep who desperately need the One True God to lovingly shepherd us.

The Good Shepherd

This comparison of two shepherds gives a life view of John chapter ten: There were two sheep ranches near each other in Africa. The one was managed by a hired hand who wasn't concerned about the sheep. He didn't care if the sheep ate, or were eaten by predators. The sheep didn't trust the hired shepherd and would flee. The other ranch was run by the owner, who lovingly shepherded his sheep. He was diligent to keep his fields full of green grass for his flock to eat, to protect them by constant surveillance, and to gently lead and guide them. The sheep knew this shepherd's voice and loved to follow him.

> *Jesus said... "I came that they may have life, and have it abundantly. I am the good shepherd; the good shepherd lays down His life for the sheep. He who is a hired hand, and not a shepherd, who is not the owner of the sheep, sees the wolf coming, and leaves the sheep and flees... He flees because he is a hired hand and is not concerned about the sheep. I am the good shepherd, and I know My own and My own know Me, even as the Father knows Me and I know the Father; and I lay down My life for the sheep... For this reason the Father loves Me, because I lay down My life so that I may take it again... My sheep hear My voice, and I know them, and they follow Me; and I give eternal life to them, and they will never perish; and no one will snatch them out of My hand. My Father, who has given them to Me, is greater than all; and no one is able to snatch them out of the Father's hand. I and the Father are one."*
> *John 10:10-30 (NASB)*

In John chapter ten, Jesus calls Himself our Good Shepherd, Who willingly gave His life for His sheep (us) so we could have eternal life, never perish, and be in His loving hands forever. While others may promise to care for us, and even give their all for us, yet as life goes, people can only do so much and some even flee. Yet, our Shepherd will never let us down or flee. He gave His life to care for us, save us from harm and to keep us securely in Him. Comforting reality living in our Shepherd's loving hands, isn't it?

Following our Good Shepherd

Our Good Shepherd, Jesus, knows His sheep (us) intimately, and He calls to us to follow Him over the many paths of life. Some of these paths can be very difficult and others not, but no matter how our path is, our Shepherd is leading us to His heavenly pasture. When your Shepherd calls to you, do you hear Him and follow, or wander without Him? Remember, His way is life eternal and life abundant; our way is, well, maybe temporarily satisfying, but after that not so much. (John 10:1-4, 10, 27-28).

To follow your Shepherd you need to be listening to His voice calling to you through His Word. If you are willing to walk close to your Shepherd by following His Word, He will lead you to His pastures, bringing a joy and contentment that only He can give. Troubles will always come and give you wobbly legs or worse, but no matter what, follow your Shepherd's voice and He will lovingly lead you through it all. Don't forget, you do have an eternity of trouble-free living just waiting for you in heaven because of your Shepherd. (Psalm 78:1, 119:105; Isaiah 40:11; Revelations 7:16-17).

Our Shepherd tenderly cares for us

I think most people know and love Psalm twenty-three; it is the Psalm which paints a vivid picture of our Shepherd's great love and care for us.

> *The LORD is my shepherd, I shall not want. He makes me lie down in green pastures; He leads me beside quiet waters. He restores my soul; He guides me in the paths of righteousness, for His name's sake. Even though I walk through the valley of the shadow of death, I fear no evil, for You are with me; Your rod and Your staff, they comfort me. You prepare a table before me in the presence of my enemies; You have anointed my head with oil; my cup overflows. Surely goodness and lovingkindness will follow me all the days of my life, and I will dwell in the house of the LORD forever. Psalm 23 (NASB)*

Psalm twenty-three describes how the LORD our Shepherd cares for us: He gives us physical nourishment and spiritual restoring. He gives us His righteousness and leads us in righteousness. His death and presence allow us to have no fear as we walk through the shadow of death and evil. Our Shepherd's rod and staff guide us, and bring us His comfort and protection. He will overflow His blessings to us here and throughout eternity. His goodness and love will be with us always, and we will literally dwell with Him forever. Yes, we surely have all we want in Jesus, our Good Shepherd. These are undoubtedly wonderful promises to ponder, aren't they?

My daughter loves Psalm twenty-three, and memorized it as a child. She is the artist who drew the sheep drawings in this book.

Our Shepherd is our peace

The world around us is full of troubles and worries, isn't it? The weeds grow, the dog barks too much, the computer has a virus, jobs disappear, cars don't work, paychecks aren't enough, accidents happen, cancer hits, people fight and so on. Will we ever have the peaceful existence we long for? Yes, in our Good Shepherd. Trust in Him. Seek Him. He promises to guide us through the worries of this world, and to lead us to a beautiful eternal serenity that He gave His life for. (Matthew 6:25-34; Revelations 7:16-17).

The fears of our world are troubling and tend to rob us of peace, don't they? There are those non-existent fears we all had as kids, and as adults we can definitely worry about things that will probably never happen. There are also those real fears that we need to deal with quite a bit, because sin has made this a fearful world. In Revelation chapter one Jesus reassuringly says, "*Do not be afraid.*" He can say this with absolute confidence - because of Who He is and what He has done for us (Revelation 1:17-18).

When the dark clouds of fear surround you, remember Who your Shepherd is, and what He has done for you. Reach out to Him in prayer. He will tenderly lead you to a peace that isn't of this world (Psalm 4:8, 139:7-12; John 14:25-27, 16:33; Philippians 4:5b-9).

~Life Application~

The end is just the beginning with God

<u>Psalm twenty-three</u> describes the One True God as our Shepherd like no other passage. *Read Psalm 23.* What do these verses tell you about God, our Shepherd? What do they say to you personally?

List some reasons you are glad Jesus is your Shepherd.

When you have the time, memorize Psalm twenty-three. I had it memorized decades ago and after I wrote today's devotion, I memorized it again. What a spiritual encouragement it has been for me to mentally meditate on each and every verse from this passage.

After studying about the One True God in this book, explain in a paragraph how you feel about Him now.

Exhortation: To be honest as I end this devotional,
I have found myself thinking, the Bible describes
the One True God as so incredible, will the readers think
He is too good to be true? Yet the truth is, our God is everything
I said He is in this book, and more. He really is all we have hoped
for, and all we ever have dreamed that the One True God
would be. Keep reading and studying God in His Word, and
the One True God will make Himself known to you in ways that
are heartwarming and truly life-changing.

Review

When you have the time, please take a few extra days and review what you have learned about the One True God. Review always helps to remember, and remembering Who God is should be paramount in all our lives.

To help with reviewing: All the characteristics and names of God in this devotional are written below. In one sentence write a description of that characteristic or name; and if you have time, describe how you have been encouraged or inspired by it.

An example from my life: God is Creator. This means He is the One Who brought forth our existence and everything else in existence by the power of His words; and He sustains that existence. When I watch nature programs on TV, I am overwhelmed with the power and wisdom it took to create such a complex world. Then I remember the Creator personally knows, loves and cares for me. Pretty amazing!

<u>Our Triune God</u>

- God the Father

- God the Son (Jesus Christ)

- God the Holy Spirit

- God is Creator

- LORD, I AM (Two names that are closely related)

- God is self-existent

- God is all-powerful

- God is eternal

- God is the source of all life

- God is sovereign

- God is holy

- God is righteous and just (Two characteristics)

- God is merciful

- High Priest

- God is good

- God is gracious/He gives grace

- God is patient

- God is unchanging

- God is faithful

- God is the true God, He is truth

- God is all-knowing

- God is all-wise

- God is always with you

- God is all-seeing and all-hearing (Two characteristics)

- God is incomprehensible

- God is kindness/kind

- God is forgiving

- God is all-loving

- God is our Eternal Father

- God is our Husband

- God is our Savior

- God is the LORD of hosts, or LORD Almighty

- Immanuel/Emmanuel

- God is our suffering Servant

- God is our Lamb

- Son of Man

- God is our good Shepherd

Thinking of Who God is, and what He has done for you, prayerfully list five ways you in turn can love and serve Him.

Nine Week Group Study Format

To group leaders: Each week seek God's presence and guidance, so you will be led by His Spirit. As the Holy Spirit leads - use the Bible passages, questions and information that are in each day's lesson, as well as the extra questions I have provided below. Establish an open and loving group atmosphere, so people will feel the freedom to share. Remember, the main purpose of this book is to get to know and love the One True God, so lead the group with this goal in mind. Be aware, Satan doesn't want us to learn about God so bathe the study group in prayer. (Satan has attacked me in various ways as I wrote this.) I would imagine you will need around 90 minutes each week for the group study, but that will depend on the number in your group.

For additional Group Study helps, go to my website: www.BecauseofGod.com

The First Week: Introduction

Preparing for the first week: The leader needs to have at least quickly reviewed the book - *The One True God and His Characteristics and Names.* Have everyone introduce themselves and share why they came. Quickly go over the 33 days in the daily devotional by reading the table of contents; then ask the group to share what characteristics and names of God they are interested in learning about, and why. Remind everyone to read, answer questions, and look up and read all Bible verses in days one through four for next week's group.

The Second Week: Days One through Four

Day 1. You Must Know the One True God
- Briefly summarize day 1, and share what encouraged you.

- Explain, why is it so important to know the One True God.

- In the Life Application section: What does it mean to you that God created you to live happily ever after?

Day 2. Thinking of God Rightly
- Briefly summarize day 2, and share what encouraged you.

- Why should you think of God rightly?

- In the Life Application section: Why do you think people want to create a false god and then worship it?

Day 3. God's Characteristics Introduced
- Briefly summarize day 3, and share what encouraged you.

- What did you learn about God's characteristics from this day?

- Reflecting on Daniel chapter two and Daniel chapter four in the Life Application section: Share one thing from these passages that motivated you to get closer to God.

- What are your thoughts about King Nebuchadnezzar and his evolving relationship with God?

Day 4. The One True God and the Trinity
- Briefly summarize day 4, and share what encouraged you.

- Do you struggle with the Doctrine of the Trinity? If so explain.

- Why would the One True God take on flesh and blood for us?

- In the Life Application section you were asked to read many Bible passages about the Trinity. Which passage enlightened you the most about the Trinity? Explain why.

- Don't forget to read, answer questions, and look up and read all Bible verses in days five through eight for next week's group.

The Third Week: Days Five through Eight

Day 5. God the Creator
- Briefly summarize day 5, and share what encouraged you.

- Romans 1:20a tells us we can see God's attributes/characteristics in His creation. In what part of creation have you seen a characteristic of God? Share one. Example: When I think of God's love, I think of Antarctica's emperor penguins and how they sacrifice for their young.

- Reflecting on Genesis chapter one, make the creation story personal. What aspects of God's creation do you appreciate the most? Examples: I grew up in Florida so I enjoy God's ocean - its sights and smells. My granddaughter loves how beautiful and unique God has made rocks, so she collects them.

- In the Life Application section: Briefly explain what God did in Genesis chapter two.

- Briefly explain what happened in Genesis 3.

Day 6. God is the LORD, I AM, the Self-Existent One
- Briefly summarize day 6, and share what encouraged you.

- Describe what it means for God to be self-existent.

- Share at least one thing from Exodus 3:1-15 about God that makes you want to know Him better.

- In the Life Application section: God the Creator and Self-Existent One chose to create us and love us because He wanted us. What does this reality mean to you?

Day 7. The One True God is All-Powerful
- Briefly summarize day 7, and share what encouraged you.

- Describe God's power.

- Share an occasion when God gave you power to overcome a situation? Example: Writing and editing this book has made me cry to God many times for the power I need to persevere in making this book publishable. Believe me, writing doesn't come easy for me. If it wasn't for God and His empowering, this book would not have been published.

- In the Life Application section: Thinking of Daniel chapter six, describe your favorite part of the story.

Day 8. God is Eternal, the Source of Life

- Briefly summarize day 8, and share what encouraged you.

- What happened to bring death to all of humankind?

- Who took on death for us so we could have life?

- Reflecting on John 11:17-45, describe your favorite part of the story.

- In the Life Application section: What are your thoughts concerning your resurrected body?

- Don't forget to read, answer questions, and look up and read all Bible verses in days nine through thirteen for next week's group.

The Fourth Week: Days Nine through Thirteen

Day 9. God is Sovereign Over All

- Quickly summarize day 9, and share what encouraged you.

- Describe God's sovereignty.

- In the Life Application: Thinking of Isaiah 40:10-28, share one thing that amazed you about God.

Day 10. The One True God is Holy
- Briefly summarize day 10, and share what encouraged you.

- Describe God's holiness and how it reacts to sin.

- Explain how people become holy to God.

- In the Life Application section: Sanctification of Christians has three parts to it. Briefly describe each part.

Day 11. The One True God is Righteous and Just
- Briefly summarize day 11, and share what encouraged you.

- Describe God's righteousness and justice?

- Sin brings punishment. Why doesn't God want to punish us? Who stopped us from being punished for our sins?

- We receive Jesus' righteousness at salvation. Does this mean we can keep on sinning? Explain why.

- In the Life Application section: Share one thing on your list from Ephesians 4:20-5:2 that you have not been doing, but want to do - to be more like Jesus.

Day 12. The One True God is Merciful
- Briefly summarize day 12, and share what encouraged you.

- Describe God's mercy.

- Share a time you gave someone mercy, and what was the result.

- Explain why it is very important that Jesus is your merciful High Priest.

- In the Life Application section: Considering John 8:1-11, share an insight you gained from the story about Jesus.

Day 13. The One True God is Good and Does Good
- Briefly summarize day 13, and share what encouraged you.

- Explain what it means to you that God is good.

- Give details of something good that has come from a trial in your own life, or from someone else's life.

- Don't forget to read, answer questions, and look up and read all Bible verses in days fourteen through seventeen for next week's group.

The Fifth Week: Days Fourteen through Seventeen

Day 14. God gives Grace, He is Gracious and Patient
- Briefly summarize day 14, and share what encouraged you.

- Compare God's grace to human grace.

- What does God's grace do for us as Christians?

- Describe God's patience.

- Are you glad God is patient? Explain why.

- In the Life Application section: Do you have bitterness in your life? If so explain. Remember, God can give you the power to give grace, and to be patient towards others.

Day 15. The One True God is Unchanging
- Briefly summarize day 15, and share what encouraged you.

- I don't take change well. I am a gal who has her routine; even good change can throw me off a bit. How does change affect you?

- What does it mean to you that God is unchanging?

Day 16. The One True God is Faithful
- Briefly summarize day 16, and share what encouraged you.

- How do you feel when someone doesn't keep their promise to you?

- Considering Jeremiah 17:5-8, why should you put your ultimate trust in God?

- In the Life Application section: Reflecting on Daniel 3:22-28, what does it mean to you that Jesus or His angel was walking with Shadrach, Meshach and Abed-nego in the furnace?

Day 17. God is Truth, He is Truthful
- Briefly summarize day 17, and share what encouraged you.

- How do you feel when someone doesn't tell you the truth?

- How important is the truth to you?

- What does it mean to you personally that God is true, and His Word is true?

- Don't forget to read, answer questions, and look up and read all Bible verses in days eighteen through twenty-one for next week's group.

The Sixth Week: Days Eighteen through Twenty-One

Day 18. The One True God is All-Knowing
- Briefly summarize day 18, and share what encouraged you.

- Compare our knowledge to God's knowledge?

- God's knowledge is found in His Word. Do you have a special way or time to study God's Word?

- In the Life Application section: What does it mean to you that God knows everything about you, and still loves you ever so much?

- Share your favorite bit of information from reading the book of Jonah.

Day 19. God is Wisdom, He is Wise
- Briefly summarize day 19, and share what encouraged you.

- Describe God's wisdom.

- We have all done unwise things. Share a time you were unwise.

- As Christians, God's wisdom lives within us. Yet to be wise, we need to do what?

- In the Life Application section: Reflecting on James 3:13-17, share one thing that you learned that made you wiser.

Day 20. The One True God is Always with You
- Briefly summarize day 20, and share what encouraged you.

- What does it mean to you that God is always with you?

- Have you ever tried to hide from God? Explain.

- In the Life Application section: Explain a time when you felt or knew God was there with you.

Day 21. The One True God is All-Seeing and All-Hearing
- Briefly summarize day 21, and share what encouraged you.

- In John chapter four, Jesus was talking with a woman. How do you think you would have felt talking to Jesus face to face?

- Since God sees and knows everything in your heart and mind, what should you be doing?

- In the Life Application section: As you can see from the story in Genesis chapter sixteen, it surprised Hagar that the One True God would appear to her - a rejected woman - to save and care for her and her descendants. But that is how our God is, isn't He? Describe one thing about God from Genesis chapter sixteen that makes you want to love Him even more.

- Don't forget to read, answer questions, and look up and read all Bible verses in days twenty-two through twenty-six for next week's group.

The Seventh Week: Days Twenty-Two through Twenty-Six

Day 22. The One true God is Incomprehensible
- Briefly summarize day 22, and share what encouraged you.

- Discuss why God is incomprehensible to us now.

- What makes the Christian God different from other gods?

- In the Life Application section: Share one thing about Jesus and his disciples that encouraged you from Mark 4:35-41.

Day 23. God is Kindness, He is kind
- Briefly summarize day 23, and share what encouraged you.

- Describe kindness.

- What has God's kindness done for you?

- What are your thoughts on God's kindness and patience waiting for you to change your mind about Jesus, so you would not perish?

- In the Life Application section: Reflecting on Ephesians 4:31-32, are you a kind or angry person?

Day 24. The One True God is the God of Forgiveness
- Briefly summarize day 24, and share what encouraged you.

- Explain God's forgiveness. What does God's forgiveness do for you?

- Explain how you should forgive others.

- Share a time in your life when someone refused to forgive you. How did it affect you?

- In the Life Application section: Do you find it hard to forgive people?

Day 25. The One True God is Love
- Briefly summarize day 25, and share what encouraged you.

- Describe in your own words God's *agape* love in the New Testament.

- Describe in your own words God's *hesed* love in the Old Testament.

- In the Life Application section: Since God loves you, does it make it easier for you to love others? Explain.

Day 26. God is All Loving and His Actions Prove It
- Briefly summarize day 26, and share what encouraged you.

- Share a time when someone stated they loved you but didn't act like it.

- Detail one action of love that God did which encourages or strengthens your love for Him.

- In the Life Application section: Did you learn a better way to show people love from 1 Corinthians 13:4-7? Explain.

- When did you realize God loved you so totally?

- Don't forget to read, answer questions, and look up and read all Bible verses in days twenty-seven through thirty for next week's group.

The Eighth Week: Days Twenty-Seven through Thirty

Day 27. The One True God is our Loving Eternal Father
- Briefly summarize day 27, and share what encouraged you.

- Define what it means to you that God is your Father?

- Describe Isaiah 49:15-16 in your own words.

- I am on a Board of an adoption agency. From the mother who wants her baby to have a better life, to the parents adopting the child - the whole situation is one of love for the baby. We could say, God loved you so much, He gave His life to adopt you. What are your thoughts on God your Father's love for you?

- From the Life Application section: Share a time you felt God your Father's comfort.

Day 28. The One True God is our Loving Husband
- Briefly summarize day 28, and share what encouraged you.

- Share one thing from this day about Jesus being your Bridegroom that makes you feel loved and wanted.

- In the Life Application section: Someday you will meet your Bridegroom, Jesus in heaven. Explain how you think you will react when you see Jesus in heaven?

Day 29. The One True God is Jesus Our Savior
- Briefly summarize day 29, and share what encouraged you.

- Describe Jesus as your Savior.

- Describe Jesus' name Immanuel.

- Describe what the LORD of hosts means.

- In the Life Application section: Reflecting on Psalm ninety-one, share one insight about God that makes you feel safe in Him.

Day 30. The One True God, Jesus, is our Suffering Servant
- Briefly summarize day 30, and share what encouraged you.

- Describe Philippians 2:6-8, in your own words.

- From the Life Application section: Share a time when someone sacrificed to serve you.

- Don't forget to read, answer questions, and look up and read all Bible verses in days thirty-one through thirty-three for next week's group.

The Ninth Week: Day Thirty-One through Thirty-Three

Day 31. Jesus the Lamb of God
- Briefly summarize day 31, and share what encouraged you.

- Do you feel loved by Jesus, because He chose to be your substitute for the punishment you deserved from your sins?

- What did Jesus accomplish by being our Lamb?

- Any thoughts on Jesus' favorite name in Revelation?

- In the Life Application section: Describe Jesus' name the Son of Man.

Day 32. The One True God Lives within Us
- Briefly summarize day 32, and share what encouraged you.

- Share a reason you are thankful the Holy Spirit is living within you.

- In the Life Application section: All my grandkids love to build things with legos. They carefully put one lego block on to another until it takes on the wonderful image of a rocket ship or tree house, etc. When we allow the Holy Spirit to lead us - God is carefully building us into His wonderful image. There are some basic Christian principles we should be doing so the Spirit can lead us. Describe what they are.

- I love to have the Spirit leading me. It's a very reassuring feeling. Give an example when you knew the Spirit was leading you.

Day 33. The One True God is our Good Shepherd
- Briefly summarize day 33, and share what encouraged you.

- Explain when you find it hard to follow your Shepherd's voice.

- Share a troubling time where you felt God's supernatural peace.

- From the Life Application section: Share your favorite verse in Psalm twenty-three and why it is. Mine is the last one, because it reminds me that God's goodness and love will always be with me. It also reminds me that I will dwell with God forever.

Footnotes

Where did I get my information for this daily devotional on God's characteristics and names? I wrote several studies - *Consider Jesus* and *A Common Sense Bible Study on Loving God, Others, and Self* to teach at our church and in the community some years back, and also the Bible study, *God Loves You and Me* which is posted on **BecauseofGod.com**. All three studies are the foundation of this daily devotional. In addition to these, I also used the resources listed for each day of this study (below) for information.

Day One: You Must Know the One True God

1. **Background of Daniel the prophet, the man who wrote the book of Daniel in the Old Testament.** Daniel was taken captive by King Nebuchadnezzar of Babylon when he was about 15 years old, with a number of other people. This was during the siege of Jerusalem in the year 605 BC. Daniel knew the One True God and served Him while he was in captivity from 605 BC until about 536 BC when he died. (This would place him under King Cyrus of the Medo-Persian Empire at the time of his death.) Daniel's godly influence changed kings and kingdoms, and God used Daniel to outline the future of our world's history for us. A few of the kings came to know the One True God through Daniel, and made him a "wise man" and /or a head ruler in their kingdoms - King Nebuchadnezzar of Babylon being the main one. When Daniel was put into the Lion's den, he was in his eighties.

Day Three: God's Characteristics Introduced

1. Wayne Grudem, **Systematic Theology,** communicable and incommunicable attributes, p156-157.

Day Four: The One True God and the Trinity

1. Wayne Grudem, **Systematic Theology,** Trinity p. 226-240.

2. Definition of Son (as in Jesus being the Son of God) - Spiros Zodhiates, **The Complete Word Study - New Testament,** definition of son, Greek word *Huios* (Strong's Word 5207), p 962.

3. **Theophany** means a direct communication or appearance by God the Son, or Jesus Christ, to human beings. These theophanies were temporary manifestations. They took place before the incarnation of Christ, which, though it began in time, will continue for all eternity.

4. The Holy Spirit is called our Helper - Spiros Zodhiates, **The Complete Word Study - New Testament,** definition of helper, Greek word *Parakletos* (Strong's number 3875), p 944.

Day Six: God is LORD, I AM, the Self-Existent One

1. Warren Baker, **The Complete Word Study - Old Testament,** definition of I AM (Strong's number 1961), p. 2311. Warren Baker, **The Complete Word Study - Old Testament,** LORD and I AM - Exodus 3:14 explained on p. 153.

2. Wayne Grudem, **Systematic Theology,** self-existent p. 160-163.

Day Ten: The One True God is Holy

1. Merrill C. Tenney, **The Zondervan, Pictorial Encyclopedia of the Bible,** Volume 3, holiness of God, p. 174-183. Warren Baker, **The Complete Word Study - Old Testament,** definition of holy, Hebrew word *Qadhosh* (Strong's number 6918), p. 2359. Spiros Zodhiates, **The Complete Word Study - New Testament,** definition of holy, Greek word *Hagios* (Strong's number 40), p. 879.

2. Wayne Grudem, **Systematic Theology,** sanctification/holiness p. 746-750.

Day Eleven: The One True God is Righteous and Just

1. Merrill C. Tenney, **The Zondervan, Pictorial Encyclopedia of the Bible,** Volume 5, righteousness of God, p. 105-115.

2. Death explained from the Bible: Death doesn't mean "extinction" as you might think, but more "a separation from." Remember, God created us eternal beings. Sleep is a term used for death, because death isn't an end (John 11:11-14). The result of sin is death (Romans 5:12; 1 Corinthians 15:56a). The punishment for sin is death (Genesis 2:16-17; Romans 6:23). Sin caused a separation with God, or <u>what is called spiritual death</u> (Isaiah 59:2). Spiritual death was immediately evidenced by Adam's and Eve's hiding from God in the garden. Death completely changed our eternal existence - instead of living with God eternally, we would live separated from Him in eternal punishment (2 Thessalonians 1:8-9). The introduction of death into our world brought awful effects to our earthly bodies as well - <u>physical death.</u> The outcome of aging, terminal illness, etc. is physical death (separation from our physical body). Physical death is a temporary separation of our soul and spirit from our body, not extinction of self; in the future, our soul and spirit will be reunited with our new resurrected body (Acts 24:15b; 1 Corinthians 15). As Christians, we are obviously still in a process of aging/dying physically, but because of Jesus we are not spiritually dead anymore. As Christians, our eternal existence will be in heaven with God (1 Thessalonians 4:13-17).

3. Kenneth S. Wuest, **Word Studies in the Greek New Testament,** Volume I, section on Ephesians 4:22-24 , p. 109-110.

Day Twelve: The One True God is Merciful

1. Spiros Zodhiates, **The Complete Word Study Dictionary - New Testament,** definition of mercy, Greek word *eleos,*. (Strong's number 1656), p 564-565.

Day Thirteen: The One True God is Good and Does Good

1. Warren Baker, **The Complete Word Study - Old Testament,** definition of good, Hebrew word *Tov* (Strong's number 2896), p. 2320.

2. Warren Baker, **The Complete Word Study - Old Testament,** definition of bad, wicked, evil, etc., Hebrew word *Ra* (Strong's number 7451), p. 2366.

Day Fourteen: God Gives Grace, He is Gracious and Patient

1. Kenneth S. Wuest, **Word Studies in the Greek New Testament,** Volume I, section on Ephesians, definition of grace, p. 20-24. Spiros Zodhiates, **The Complete Word Study Dictionary - New Testament,** definition of grace, Greek word *charis,* (Strong's number 5485), p 1469-1471.

Day Fifteen: The One True God is Unchanging

1. John F. Walvoord & Roy B. Zuck, **The Bible Knowledge Commentary Old Testament Edition,** Exodus 32, p. 156.

Day Seventeen: God is Truth, He is Truthful

1. Josh McDowell, **The New Evidence that Demands a Verdict,** Part 1 - The Case for the Bible & Part 2 - The Case for Jesus.

Day Nineteen: God is Wisdom, He is Wise

1. Wayne Grudem, **Systematic Theology,** Wisdom p. 193-195.

2. **Anthropic Principle** - Our universe appears as if it is designed for man. It is "fine tuned" for the existence of man and life. Thomas M. Crawford.

Day Twenty-Three: God is Kindness, He is Kind

1. Spiros Zodhiates, **The Complete Word Study Dictionary - New Testament,** definition of kindness/kind, Greek words *agathosunes* & *Chrestotes* (Strong's number 19 also 5544), p. 63 also 1482.

2. Spiros Zodhiates, **The Complete Word Study Dictionary - New Testament,** definition of repentance, Greek word *Metanoia* (Strong's number 3341), p. 970-972.

Day Twenty-Four: The One True God is the God of Forgiveness

1. Spiros Zodhiates, **The Complete Word Study Dictionary - New Testament,** definition of forgiveness, Greek words *Aphesis/Aphiemi* (Strong's number 859 also 863), p. 296-297 also 299-300.

Day Twenty-Five: The One True God is Love

1. Spiros Zodhiates, **The Complete Word Study - New Testament,** definition of love, Greek words *Agape* and *Agapao* (Strong's numbers 25 also 26), p. 878. Kenneth S. Wuest, **Word Studies in the Greek New Testament,** Volume I, section on Ephesians, definition of love/*agape*, p.65 & 131. Kenneth S. Wuest, **Word Studies in the Greek New Testament,** Volume III, definition of love/*agapao*, p.60-61. Leon Morris, **Tyndale New Testament Commentaries,** 1 Corinthians, definition of love/*agape*, p. 176-177.

2. Warren Baker, **The Complete Word Study - Old Testament,** definition of lovingkindness etc., Hebrew word *chesedh/hesed* (Strong's number 2617), p. 2317.

Day Twenty-Seven: The One True God is our Loving Eternal Father

1. Wayne Grudem, **Systematic Theology,** Roles in Trinity p. 248-252.

Day Twenty-Nine: The One True God is Jesus our Savior

1. Spiros Zodhiates, **The Complete Word Study Dictionary - New Testament,** definition of Savior, Greek word *soter* (Strong's number 4990), p 1360.

2. Warren Baker, **The Complete Word Study - Old Testament,** definition of host for LORD of Hosts, Hebrew word *tsava* (Strong's number 6635), p. 2357.

Day Thirty: The One True God, Jesus, is our Suffering Servant

1. Kenneth S. Wuest, **Word Studies in the Greek New Testament,** Volume II, section on Philippians 2:6-8, p. 62-70. Spiros Zodhiates, **The Complete Word Study Dictionary - New Testament,** definition of emptied, Greek word *keno* (Strong's number 2758), p 857-858.

Day Thirty-One: Jesus the Lamb of God

1. William Hendriksen, **New Testament Commentary - Matthew,** Matthew 8:20 - Son of Man defined, p 403-407.

Day Thirty-Two: The One True God Lives within Us

1. **Holy Spirit Sealed** - Kenneth S. Wuest, **Word Studies in the Greek New Testament,** Volume I, section on Ephesians 4:13, p 49.

2. **Holy Spirit Pledge** (Ephesians 4:14) - Warren W. Wiersbe, **The Bible Exposition Commentary,** Volume 2, p 13.

For God so loved the world, that He gave His only begotten Son, that whoever believes in Him shall not perish, but have eternal life. For God did not send the Son into the world to judge the world, but that the world might be saved through Him. He who believes in Him is not judged; he who does not believe has been judged already, because he has not believed in the name of the only begotten Son of God. John 3:16-18

About the Author

Gini Crawford has been a Christian since 1971. She has had the privilege of teaching and shepherding women in God's Word through church ministries and in the community for the last 40-some years. Since 2007, Gini has had a ministry called Because of God Ministries. The foundation of the ministry is a popular Christian website with free Bible resources (devotionals and studies) that are Biblical with a little humor thrown in. The website is: **www.BecauseofGod.com.** Several organizations are using her teachings from Because of God Ministries. A ministry in India, New Hope India Ministries, translates her devotions into the language of the area for use in their women's ministries.

Gini received her Masters in Social Work (MSW) - Counseling in 2004. Her area of expertise was sexual assault counseling. She stays active in her career field as a Board Member of an adoption agency and volunteering in the community for various things. Since 2009 Gini has managed a number of political campaigns in Southern Arizona. Because of running political campaigns, Gini took some time off writing for Because of God Ministries. Since God has literally cleared her schedule, she is back writing now.

Gini and her husband, Tom, have been married 45 years. They have three adult children, all married, and seven terrific grandchildren. Gini's hobbies are: walking (and talking to God), tennis, bicycling and swimming (to burn those calories), and watching grandkids.

A Personal Note

Please keep on getting to know and love the One True God (Who loves us beyond human reason) from His Word! It is a life long journey that I have been on now for over 49 years ... and don't regret a moment of it. I want to thank you for hanging in there with me. It took a desire to know God to persevere through 33 days of my writings.

See you in heaven before our God!

gini

Made in the USA
Monee, IL
11 July 2022

99485772R00131